Ricardian Poetry

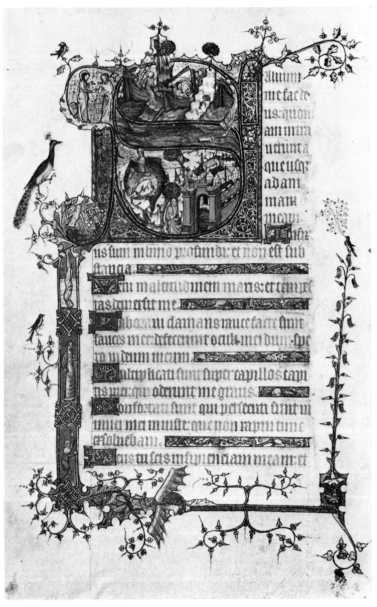

From an English manuscript of about 1370
[see note on the Frontispiece]

J. A. Burrow
Jesus College, Oxford

Ricardian Poetry

Chaucer, Gower, Langland and the *Gawain* Poet

Routledge & Kegan Paul

London

First published 1971
by Routledge and Kegan Paul Ltd
Broadway House
68–74 Carter Lane
London, EC4V 5EL
Printed in Great Britain
and set in 11 on 12 point Ehrhardt
by Ebenezer Baylis and Son Limited
The Trinity Press, Worcester, and London
© J. A. Burrow 1971

ISBN: 0 7100 7031 4

Contents

Preface

The poems discussed in this book are quoted from the following editions: Chaucer, *Complete Works* ed. F. N. Robinson, 2nd ed., Cambridge, Mass., 1957; Gower, *Confessio Amantis* ed. G. C. Macaulay, E.E.T.S. e.s. 81, 82 (1900, 1901); Langland, *Piers Plowman*, B-text, ed. W. W. Skeat, E.E.T.S. o.s. 38 (1869); *Sir Gawain and the Green Knight* ed. J. R. R. Tolkien and E. V. Gordon, 2nd ed. revised by Norman Davis, Oxford, 1967; *Pearl* ed. E. V. Gordon, Oxford, 1953; *Patience* ed. J. J. Anderson, Manchester, 1969; *Purity* ed. R. J. Menner, New Haven, Conn., 1920. The treatment of spelling in quotations is explained in note 27 on p. 145.

Students at the Yale Graduate School and at Oxford have helped me with suggestions and criticisms. I am also indebted to Nicholas Jacobs and George Hersey for help and advice. My debt to earlier critics of the four poets under discussion will be obvious on every page. I am sorry that Dr A. C. Spearing's book *The Gawain Poet* appeared too late for me to make use of it here.

Jesus College, Oxford

Ricardian Poetry

Note on the Frontispiece

The page illustrated comes from the Vienna Psalter (Vienna, Nationalbib., Cod. 1826*). This manuscript was made for Humphrey de Bohun, 7th Earl of Hereford, shortly before his death in 1372–3. It therefore belongs to the earliest part of the period 1370–1400 with which this book deals.

The text is the opening of Psalm 68 in the Vulgate version (number 69 in the Authorized Version), beginning *Salvum me fac, Deus*: 'Save me, O God; for the waters are come in unto my soul. I sink in deep mire, where there is no standing: I am come into deep waters, where the floods overflow me. . . '. As was customary, the initial S of this psalm is decorated with scenes from the story of Jonah and the whale. At the top left, in the separate compartment, God speaks to Jonah. In the upper lobe of the S, the story is continued in three scenes. On the left, Jonah enters the ship; in the centre, the ship loses its mast in the storm; on the right, a man lowers Jonah into the sea. In the sea, which is represented by the crossband of the S, swims the great fish. The lower lobe of the S portrays, on the left, Jonah emerging from the fish, and on the right, Jonah sitting outside Nineveh under a tree.

Stylistically, the page is an example of the manner most commonly found in English illuminated MSS. of the later fourteenth century. Work in this 'English style' (as Miss Rickert calls it) has a prima facie claim to be compared with the English poetry of the same period, which I shall call 'Ricardian'. (See Introduction.) Like the Ricardian poets, the painters of the English style lack the up-to-date elegance and polish of their French contemporaries. Although Italian influence is strong in some Bohun MSS., as it is in some of Chaucer's poems, the Bohun style has its roots in older native traditions, just as Chaucer's does. Even Chaucer, the most sophisticated and cosmopolitan of the Ricardian poets, remains faithful in his fashion to the traditions of English poetry. (Chapter 1.)

The initial S on this page, with its spirited little scenes packed into the ornamental framework of the capital, illustrates what Miss Rickert describes as a characteristically English taste for 'combining a pleasing overall design with the lively interest and variety of a narrative'. This combination is matched in the poetry of the Ricardian period. Chaucer, Gower, the *Gawain* poet and Langland all cultivate 'the lively interest and variety of a narrative'. They are all essentially story-telling poets. At the same time, they regularly enclose their stories within frames, often richly decorated, and so produce 'a pleasing overall design'. (Chapter 2.)

The treatment of the human figures in the page, both in the initial and in the borders, is expressive, sometimes humorous, and quite unmonumental. This matches the essentially unheroic treatment of man in Ricardian poetry. The portrait of Jonah in the initial (especially his comical complacency as he sits under the tree) may be compared with the portrait of Jonah in the *Gawain* poet's humorous and spirited version of the same story in *Patience*. (Chapter 3.)

References

James, M. R. and Millar, E. G., *The Bohun Manuscripts,* Roxburghe Club, Oxford, 1936: Plate XLV, described on p. 38.

Rickert, M., *The Reconstructed Carmelite Missal,* London, 1952: especially 71–6.

Rickert, M., *Painting in Britain: The Middle Ages,* 2nd ed., Harmondsworth, 1965: especially 149–50.

Salter, E., 'The Alliterative Revival', *Modern Philology,* lxiv (1966–7), 146–50, 233–7.

Robertson, D. W., Jr., *A Preface to Chaucer,* Princeton, 1963: 221–4, 279, 282.

Introduction

Ricardian Poetry

Most of the best poetry surviving from the Middle English period belongs to the fourteenth century. In the later part of this century English poetry seems to have enjoyed one of its periods of florescence. The evidence for the dating of individual poems, such as it is, points to the last years of King Edward III (reigned 1327–77) and the reign of King Richard II (1377–99) as the time of greatest distinction. Here, in the space of thirty years from the plague of 1369 to the accession of Henry IV, belong the works of Chaucer, Gower, Langland and the anonymous author (or possibly authors) of *Sir Gawain and the Green Knight*, *Pearl* and the other poems in the manuscript Cotton Nero A.x.[1]

The individual characteristics and merits of these four poets – with the possible exception of Gower – have been adequately studied and appreciated. Their common characteristics, however, are little recognized. They do not belong together, in the established history of English poetry, as representatives of a single period, like Pope and Swift, or Tennyson and Browning. Despite its fertility, indeed, the age of Chaucer and Langland has failed to achieve the full status of a literary 'period'. The best evidence of this failure is that the age lacks any name beyond the merest chronological labels. To call Pope an 'eighteenth-century' poet or Tennyson a 'Victorian' is more than just to date them. Such terms are pregnant with a certain elementary but indispensable sense of period. In a literary context they will suggest certain norms – of style, theme, convention, philosophy, etc. – to which even the most fastidious and sceptical critics refer, if only to deny their adequacy ('Tennyson is much more than a conventionally "Victorian" poet'). In the case of Chaucer and his contemporaries, the sense of such norms is lacking. Hence to call Chaucer a 'fourteenth-century' poet means less than to call Pope an 'eighteenth-century' one. The description fails to set up any distinct literary (as opposed to historical or linguistic) expectations. The term 'fourteenth-century' is barely more than a chronological marker; and it is hard to find a more expressive term in current usage.

In the absence of a period-name I have found it necessary to invent one, or rather to borrow it from the historians. Histories of this period derive from the name of Richard II the convenient epithet 'Ricardian'; and it is this epithet that I hope to establish in literary usage. Some people object to the use of regnal labels in literary history. Henri Peyre says that they represent 'la manière la plus élémentaire et la plus naïve de désigner les auteurs'.[2] But a period needs a name; and I cannot think of a better one for this period than 'Ricardian'. Admittedly, the term is not perfectly apt. Richard came to the throne inconveniently late for our purposes (though for no other); and his tastes in literature seem to have run more to French than to English.[3] Gower, according to his own account, undertook *Confessio Amantis* at the King's command; but the only work of Chaucer's which can be directly connected with Richard is the ballade *Lak of Stedfastnesse*.[4] Richard was a man of cultivated taste; but he was never, despite his absolutist leanings, an arbiter or cynosure of poets, in the manner of Renaissance monarchs such as Elizabeth I. Hence he does not represent, as Elizabeth does, a natural centre and symbol for the literature of his day. Yet many other period-names function effectively as literary terms despite similar disadvantages.[5]

There are, needless to say, good reasons why the later fourteenth century has failed to achieve the full status of a literary period. Some of these reasons are intrinsic, others extrinsic. The most important of the intrinsic reasons appear as soon as one sets *Sir Gawain and the Green Knight* down beside Chaucer's *Troilus and Criseyde*. Both are polite works, recognizing the same international standards of courtly conduct; but they do not speak the same polite language. We observe differences of dialect – phonological, morphological, lexical – of a kind that we are not accustomed to in later English poetry, or in Anglo-Saxon poetry for that matter. This 'gret diversite in Englissh and in writyng of oure tonge' of which Chaucer complains towards the end of *Troilus* (v. 1793–4) impairs the unity of the period. It must have prevented contemporaries from fully understanding and appreciating work being done in dialect-areas other than their own. It also presents the modern reader with a very heterogeneous body of texts.

Equally unusual and daunting are the differences of metrical convention which separate *Gawain* and *Troilus*. Chaucer's rhyme royal and the Northern poet's alliterative verse are not simply two different metrical forms: they represent quite distinct ways of composing English verse, as the Spenserian stanza and Shakespeare's blank verse, say, do not. A passage from one recent theoretical essay on metre will suggest just how fundamental this distinction is:

> There are in fact two main kinds of stress metre in English: the very old (and recently revived) metre of strong stress with indeterminate or relatively indeterminate number of syllables between the stresses, and the other metre, of the great English art tradition (Chaucer to Tennyson), which is a syllable-stress metre, that is, a metre of counted syllables and of both major and minor stresses.[6]

Thus the great metrical divide in English poetry runs clean through the middle of Ricardian poetry, separating Langland and the *Gawain* poet from Chaucer and Gower.

It would be easier to grasp some unity in this diversity if the writers themselves were more ready to help, with comments on their own aims and principles or with criticism of the achievements of their contemporaries. The age had, of course, no organs of critical opinion, and it produced no cardinal critical document – no *Deffence et Illustration* or Preface to the *Lyrical Ballads*. The Alliterative Revival, whatever else it may have been, was not a literary 'movement' in the modern sense; and the 'London School' (comprising chiefly Chaucer and Gower) is little more than a convenient fiction of the literary historian. We know that Chaucer and Gower knew each other; and their literary relationship, though not documented like that of Wordsworth and Coleridge, can be imagined with the help of a few passages such as *Confessio Amantis* viii. 2941*–2957* and *Troilus* v. 1856–9.[7] But what did either of them know or think of their fellow-citizen Langland? And could either of them have appreciated the *Gawain* poet? We can only guess.[8] Chaucer's position in regard to the poetry which he imitates in *Sir Thopas* may be inferred – with due caution – from that remarkable parody. But *Sir Thopas* throws no light on the chief mystery of the age: the relations between alliterative and non-alliterative poetry. The statement by Chaucer's Parson later in the *Canterbury Tales* (x. 43) that he 'kan nat geeste "rum, ram, ruf," by lettre' has led some to suppose that alliterative verse was regarded in the metropolis as a provincial aberration; but such a hypothesis, based on such a tiny and questionable fragment of evidence (the speaker is the Parson not Chaucer, and he goes on to say that he holds rhyme 'but litel bettre'), just shows how desperate is the shortage of literary comment in the documents of this period.[9] Equally shaky is the hypothesis put forward by J. R. Hulbert, that alliterative verse was cultivated by the barons, in the spirit of *kulturkampf*, as a counterblast to the Frenchified verse of the royal court.[10] The fact is that the two main bodies of Ricardian poetry did not, so far as our knowledge goes, define themselves through any process of public debate, as the Lake and Cockney poets defined themselves in a later age. Indeed, the two 'schools' present themselves to us as largely unconscious of each other. This has been one of the chief obstacles in the way of a truly synoptic view of the period.

In part, then, the modern failure to see Ricardian poetry whole stems from the nature, the polycentricity, of the period itself. Literature was still to some extent, though decreasingly, a local affair. The national literary scene had not yet formed. Besides these intrinsic reasons, however, there are others which lie outside the period, in later developments both linguistic and literary. As a result of these developments, the individual Ricardian poets enjoyed posthumous fortunes so various that it is now difficult, even under academic conditions, to treat them alike.

The establishment in the fifteenth century of the London dialect as the standard language of a by-now national literature favoured the fortunes of those fourteenth-century writers, notably Chaucer and Gower, who had used that form of English or something like it, as against those such as the *Gawain* poet who had not. If Chester rather than London had become the capital centre of England, no doubt the *Gawain* poet would immediately have been acknowledged a national classic, and a north-western Caxton would have rushed his work into print. As things were, however, he fell into oblivion. His work did influence some later alliterative writers, and it was still being read in his own part of the country as late as the early sixteenth century;[11] but he had not at any time, apparently, achieved more than a limited currency, and by Elizabethan times he must count as unknown. The single manuscript in which his works survive, B.M. Cotton Nero A.x., is also the only manuscript of which there is any record. After being in the library of an Elizabethan antiquary, Henry Savile of Bank in Yorkshire, it was acquired by Sir Robert Cotton and thence passed to the British Museum. Thomas Warton, author of the *History of English Poetry* (1774–81), was acquainted with the manuscript, and he quoted short passages from the poems which we now call *Pearl* and *Purity*; but Richard Price, who in 1824 published a new edition of Warton's *History*, was apparently the first person in modern times to recognize the significance of its contents. The first passage from *Sir Gawain and the Green Knight* ever to be printed (ll. 20–36) appeared at that late date in Price's Warton.[12] Fifteen years later the whole of *Sir Gawain* was made public by Sir F. Madden, in a collection of old poems about Gawain prepared, with the encouragement of Sir Walter Scott, for the Bannatyne Club (1839). Twenty-five years later the newly-formed Early English Text Society devoted the first of its publications (*Early English Alliterative Poems*, 1864) to an edition by R. Morris of the other three poems in the manuscript. Thus *Pearl, Patience* and *Purity* were printed for the first time entire and became generally available together with *Sir Gawain* (re-edited by Morris for another E.E.T.S. volume), at least to the learned world.

The work of the *Gawain* poet, then, shared the fate of much medieval literature. It disappeared completely from the literary scene, only to be restored by the scholarship of the Romantic period. The case of Langland is different. *Piers Plowman* seems to have been widely read both in its own day and in the fifteenth century (when its language, unlike that of the Cotton Nero MS., must have been quite easy for most readers to understand). The fifty-one manuscripts of the poem present a striking contrast with the single manuscripts in which the works of so many other alliterative poets survive.[13] Langland is, indeed, the only alliterative poet (Old or Middle English) who has at no time disappeared from the English literary scene. As Skeat says, 'the work, though seldom well known, was at no time quite forgotten'.[14] The printed editions (based on manuscripts of the B-version) of Crowley (1550) and Rogers (1561) made him available to Elizabethan and Jacobean readers, many of whom saw in him a precursor of their own Protestant faith. In the epilogue to his *Shepheardes Calender* Spenser couples *Piers* with Chaucer's work as high models to imitate; and at about the same time Puttenham, in his *Arte of English Poesie*, speaks of Langland as a satirist in the same breath with Lucilius and Juvenal. Even Milton ranks him with the Latin and Italian satirists as a model of satirical writing.[15] Although Langland was not printed again, except in extracts, after the editions of Crowley and Rogers until 1813, when Whitaker produced a new edition based on a C-manuscript, his reputation as a black-letter satirist survived through the seventeenth and eighteenth centuries. Thomas Warton devotes to his work a whole section of the *History*, in which he censures Langland's 'affectation of obsolete English', but praises his satiric verve as well as his picturesque humour and imaginative sublimity.[16]

Yet it cannot be said that even Langland, despite his continuing reputation as a satirist, ever achieved quite his due place in readers' consciousness of the Ricardian age. This consciousness was chiefly formed by the judgments of writers in the fifteenth and sixteenth centuries who owed relatively little to Langland or to the traditions which he represented. For these writers and their readers it was Chaucer and Gower – the 'London School' – who really counted. Chaucer and Gower were the *migliori fabbri* who had established the new style of polite poetry in English; and their names were commonly coupled together in eulogistic references by poets such as Lydgate in England and Dunbar in Scotland.[17] Caxton printed works of both of them, and other editions (frequent in the case of Chaucer) sustained their reputations throughout the sixteenth century. The edition of *Confessio Amantis* by Berthelette (first 1532, second 1554) deserves special mention, since modern readers often fail to appreciate the extent of Gower's reputation in earlier periods. In his address to the reader, Berthelette speaks of Gower as 'this mooste plesunt and easy auctor'; and in his dedication he represents him as a model of good English, copious without affectation, who can teach a modern writer 'to wryte counnyngly and to garnysshe his sentencis in our vulgar tonge'.[18] It is not surprising, therefore, that Shakespeare used and imitated 'ancient Gower' in *Pericles*, or that Ben Jonson cited more examples from Gower than from any other author in his *English Grammar* (1640).

In Sidney's *Apologie for Poetrie* Chaucer and Gower figure as the joint founders of English poetry: 'So among the Romans were *Livius Andronicus* and *Ennius*. So in the Italian language the first that made it aspire to be a Treasure-house of Science were the poets *Dante*, *Boccace* and *Petrarch*. So in our English were *Gower* and *Chawcer*.'[19] Chaucer and Gower occupy the same position in Puttenham's *Arte of English Poesie* (1589):

6

I will not reach above the time of king *Edward* the third and
Richard the second for any that wrote in English meeter,
because before their times, by reason of the late Normane
conquest, which had brought into this Realme much alteration
both of our langage and lawes, and there withall a certain
martiall barbarousnes, whereby the study of all good learning
was so much decayd as long time after no man or very few
entended to write any laudable science: so as beyond that time
there is litle or nothing worth commendation to be founde
written in this arte. And those of the first age were *Chaucer*
and *Gower*, both of them, as I suppose, Knightes. After whom
followed *Iohn Lydgate,* the monke of Bury, and that nameles,
who wrote the *Satyre* called Piers Plowman; next him followed
Harding, the Chronicler; then, in king *Henry* th'eights time,
Skelton, (I wot not for what great worthines) surnamed the
Poet *Laureat*. In the latter end of the same kings raigne sprong
up a new company of courtly makers, of whom Sir *Thomas
Wyat* th'elder and *Henry* Earle of Surrey were the two
chieftaines.[20]

Langland has a place in this interesting passage, but he is relegated
to the second, Lydgatian generation, leaving Sir Geoffrey Chaucer
and Sir John Gower to represent without rivals the 'first age'. Just
as Wyatt and Surrey were the two 'chieftaines' of the 'new company
of courtly makers' under Henry VIII, Puttenham implies, so Chaucer
and Gower were the two chieftains of the first such company under
Edward III and Richard II. The shaping spirit of the literary historian is at work in these symmetries.

By Dryden's time Chaucer and Gower had become not only
knights but poets laureate as well. The patent of 1670 which confirmed Dryden in the office of laureate speaks of him as enjoying
'the rights, privileges, benefits and advantages thereunto belonging
as fully and amply as Sir Geoffrey Chaucer Knight, Sir John Gower
Knight, John Leland Esquire . . .'.[21] This document expresses a
widely-held belief about the beginnings of the laureateship which,
se non è vero, è ben trovato. A laureate is a poet of learning and polish
patronized by royalty and recognized as the representative in his age
of the great tradition of his people's poetry. In such a laureate
succession only Chaucer and Gower could be considered worthy to
represent the age of Richard.[22]

A century later even Thomas Warton, a literary historian of catholic tastes and wide reading, remains faithful to this idea of a laureate succession in English poetry beginning with Chaucer and Gower. Langland may be sublime, but only Chaucer and Gower in their age were truly civilized poets: 'If Chaucer had not existed, the compositions of John Gower, the next poet in succession, would alone have been sufficient to rescue the reigns of Edward the Third and Richard the Second from the imputation of barbarism. His education was liberal and uncircumscribed, his course of reading extensive, and he tempered his severer studies with a knowledge of life.'[23] Warton thus states in the language of his time a view of the Ricardian period very like Puttenham's.

The picture has changed somewhat since Warton's time. On the one hand, Gower, whose reputation never matched Chaucer's, has generally failed to arouse the interest of readers, despite the excellent editing of G. C. Macaulay and the eloquent advocacy of C. S. Lewis.[24] Coleridge called him 'the almost worthless Gower', and classed him among 'the lengthy poets who . . . make drossy lead as ductile as pure gold'.[25] On the other hand, through the labours of Warton's learned successors – Madden, Wright, Skeat and the rest – much good poetry lying outside the laureate tradition has been made available to readers, often (as in the case of the *Gawain* poet) for the first time. Yet we still have not brought our view of the period into a single focus. Thus Chaucer, as the representative of the 'great English art tradition (Chaucer to Tennyson)', is often segregated in the syllabus of university Schools of English from his less brilliant contemporaries, who are treated separately under the heading 'Middle English' or, less formally, 'Language'. The same difference of treatment appears in such small but significant matters as the orthography of printed texts. The symbol þ (thorn), for example, is often used alongside *th* in manuscripts of the period. Most editions of Middle English texts – the standard editions of *Gawain* and *Pearl*, for example – preserve this thorn as a matter of course; but editions of Chaucer dispense with it so regularly that readers find it hard to believe that Chaucer was ever acquainted with this fragment of runic antiquity. In the same way, Macaulay in his E.E.T.S. edition of Gower uses *th* for the þ of the manuscripts, whereas Skeat in his E.E.T.S. edition of Langland does not.[26] The result of this and other divergences in the editorial handling of the manuscripts is that the texts of Gower and Chaucer are given a relatively modern appearance, while those of their contemporaries are left under 'the imputation of barbarism'; and this in turn helps to perpetuate our essentially bifocal view of the period.[27]

Posterity, then, has not treated the Ricardian poets alike. This unlikeness of fortune is itself a fact which we cannot ignore any more than we can ignore the intrinsic differences of dialect and metre discussed earlier. The *Gawain* poet uses a form of English which puts him beyond at least the instant comprehension of readers accustomed to the standard language, the *volgare illustre*, of English literature in its main tradition. That is a fact. It is also a fact that he cannot claim to count historically in that tradition, as Chaucer counts, by virtue of the admiration and imitation of his successors. In that way he lacks consequence. Facts such as these cannot be challenged, however enthusiastic one may be about a poet's merits. Only when the whole metropolitan, laureate or art tradition has ceased altogether to command readers will they begin to feel themselves equidistant from *Troilus and Criseyde* and *Sir Gawain and the Green Knight*. That day still seems rather remote, in England at least, despite a growing eclecticism in literary taste which has led to increased use of non-standard English in poetry, and to the revived practice of alliterative verse together with other ways of writing alien to the 'great English art tradition'.

In the meantime, the present book represents an attempt simply to look at the four chief poets of Richard's reign as a group. I have tried to treat their works alike and together, as if they were pictures hanging round the walls of a room devoted, in an imaginary museum, to the 'Ricardian School'. I have gone round the rich and varied, though rather small, collection, looking for common features of style, subject, treatment, mood and construction. Some readers of the discussions which follow may feel that I have persuaded myself to see common features which are not there, others that I have chosen the wrong features to emphasize. It is not to be expected that any one reader's characterization of a whole literary period will impose itself on his contemporaries, let alone his successors. Our judgment of what is distinctive in a period, for one thing, depends on what we are wanting to distinguish it from; and that in turn depends largely on our own particular reading and interests. I hope, however, that my account of the matter will start a debate from which may emerge some clearer sense of what the poetry of this age is like. The age may turn out not to have been a 'period', in the full literary sense, at all; but even that result would have its own interest.

In conclusion, two explanations. First, I do not claim that all the features discussed are common to all the works under discussion. The common features, or norms, of a literary period do not, even in France, manifest themselves with that kind of regularity. As René Wellek says: 'A period is not an ideal type or an abstract pattern or a series of class concepts, but a time section, dominated by a whole system of norms, which no work of art will ever realize in its entirety.'[28] Second, I make no attempt to give a comprehensive account of the poetry written in England between 1370 and 1400, still less to construct (if that is indeed possible) a literary history of the age.[29] I exclude the Latin and French poems of Gower, because several important features of 'Ricardian poetry' derive from characteristics specifically of the English language at that time, and this is not the place to demonstrate the absence of these features in Gower's non-English writings. I also exclude from direct consideration a good deal of vernacular poetry which may be held (though there are often uncertainties of date) to fall within the limits of the period. Some of the poets are simply not good enough to make any contribution to the main creative effort of their time. Thomas Chestre, the (probably) late fourteenth-century author of *Launfal* and also, perhaps, of *Libeaus Desconus* and the southern *Octavian*, is a lively rhymer in the manner of the minstrels; and Sir John Clanvowe, probable author of the *Boke of Cupide*, is a competent imitator, in a more courtly vein, of his contemporary Chaucer; but neither Chestre nor Clanvowe can claim a place in the present company.[30] Other poets of greater distinction are also excluded, for various reasons which usually include difficulties of dating. To some of these poets, it would seem, period norms just do not apply: one would not expect traditional ballads to exhibit Ricardian characteristics. Other writers, such as the author of the alliterative *Morte Arthure*, may find their place in a view of the period more comprehensive than mine.

Chapter one

Ricardian Style

It seems most unlikely that Langland, Chaucer, Gower and the *Gawain* poet shared any ideal of English style distinctive enough to count as 'Ricardian'. Such common ideals of style as they did recognize were no doubt just those taught by grammarians and rhetoricians in Europe throughout the Middle Ages.[1] There can be no question, therefore, of identifying in their work a consciously cultivated Ricardian style, as critics have identified a metaphysical style in the works of Donne and Herbert. Indeed, it might be argued that the differences in style between, say, Langland and Chaucer are more evident than the similarities. A common style is certainly harder to see in the English poetry of the age than it is in the painting or sculpture. The regional, decentralized life of the times makes itself felt in the poetry, especially in its verbal texture, more insistently than in those arts which do not use language. Poets still wrote in their own local dialects, not in a standard literary dialect; and the northerly English of the *Gawain* poet, with its distinctive features of vocabulary and sound, differed from Chaucer's London English in its expressive possibilities. Again, the coexistence in the period of two such different traditions of verse-writing as the alliterative and the non-alliterative or 'metrical' told against the realizing of any common stylistic ideal, even supposing that such an ideal could have been formed by poets who were not, generally speaking, in communication with each other.

What follows in this chapter, then, is not the description of a single developed and clearly-articulated style which can stand with the metaphysical or Augustan styles as one of the stable achievements of English poetry. I shall attempt a theory rather than a description; and I shall try to show that the common, the Ricardian, characteristics in the style of these poets reside, not in any stable set of particular features such as a 'school' might cultivate, but rather in a relationship between the poet and his medium. The terms of this relationship are dictated, very largely, by the history of English language and literature in the fourteenth century. Round about the middle of this century, as historians agree, the language entered a new phase of growth and expansion during which it was to take over most of the functions – in polite conversation, scholastic instruction, learned disquisition – previously performed in England as elsewhere by French or Latin.[2] But the idioms of English poetry current in the 1350's and 1360's still belonged to an earlier, simpler age. Neither the alliterative traditions of the north and west nor the metrical traditions of the east and south could offer a poetic vernacular adapted to such purposes as a new generation of poets were beginning to conceive.[3] These poets might, accordingly, have tried to break away completely from the past; but they did not do so. Even Chaucer, whose knowledge not only of French and Latin but also of the new Italian poetry must have made him acutely aware of the insufficiencies of *Guy of Warwick* and *Sir Orfeo*, cultivated an English style which is much more traditional than many people realize. This conservatism is a source of strength in his work, as it is also in the work of the *Gawain* poet; but it also brought with it problems, constraints and a certain weakness. For the insufficiencies were real, and they forced Ricardian poets into many improvisations and accommodations, ironies and silences, some of which I shall attempt to illustrate in the following pages.

I

When the hero of Chaucer's tale of *Sir Thopas* is preparing to arm for his battle against the giant he calls for entertainment:

> 'Do come,' he seyde, 'my mynstrales,
> And geestours for to tellen tales,
>   Anon in myn armynge,
> Of romances that been roiales,
> Of popes and of cardinales,
>   And eek of love-likynge.'
>
> (*Canterbury Tales* vii. 845–50)

Some recent writers on English poetry in the later Middle Ages have attacked what they call the 'romantic fiction' of the minstrel.[4] They point out rightly that the term 'minstrel' itself in fourteenth-century English usually, as in the passage from *Sir Thopas*, seems to refer to a musical rather than a literary entertainer;[5] and they question whether the other kind of entertainer mentioned by Chaucer, the 'geestour' (from Old French *geste*, an exploit or a romance of exploits), would normally have had anything to do with the composition of the romances which he recited.[6] Even as a reciter his importance has been questioned. Scenes such as that described in *Sir Thopas* already in Chaucer's time belonged to the past, it is suggested, because the spread of literacy had by then freed most people from dependence on the professional performer. A 'geestour' (or 'disour' as he was also called) would no longer be necessary in a household such as that of Criseyde in *Troilus*, where 'the geste of the siege of Thebes' is read aloud by a handmaiden to entertain her mistress (ii. 82 ff).[7]

Such arguments betray in places a distinct counter-romantic bias. The modern academic is just as capable of seeing in the past what he wants to see, or what he is accustomed to, as was the antiquary of Romantic times. If the 'geestour' or 'disour' was as unimportant a person as these writers suggest, it is hard to understand why the sources mention him so often.[8] Yet one must concede that the production and consumption of the Middle English romances is much too varied and complex a matter to be covered by any single hypothesis such as that of 'minstrelsy'. Poems like *Guy of Warwick* and *Libeaus Desconus* must have been produced some of them by 'disours', some by 'clerks' or literary men, and some by persons who, like the *clérigos ajuglarados* or 'minstrelized clerks' of medieval Spain, simply do not fit into any category.[9] As for 'consumption', a single popular poem like *Guy* was no doubt consumed in a multitude of different ways on different occasions: the clever member of a family or household would have read it, sometimes aloud to others, sometimes in private and even silently; a 'disour' would have recited it to an audience of patrons, sometimes from a manuscript copy, sometimes from memory; and so on. The important fact for our present purposes, however, is that the Middle English romances, however various their history and circumstances, exhibit a relatively unvarying, indeed an unmistakable, style – that style which Chaucer imitates in *Sir Thopas*; and unquestionably this style belongs not to literary men but to 'geestours', 'disours' or (to depart from fourteenth-century usage) minstrels. Partly, no doubt, because they still wrote mainly for the ear rather than for the eye, 'literary' authors of romances continued to cultivate a minstrel manner, full of tags and formulas, appeals to the audience and heavily marked narrative transitions.[10] For the purposes of a descriptive study of styles, therefore, the literary status of these authors is of very little consequence, even where it can be proved. They might just as well have been minstrels for all the difference it makes to their way of writing.[11]

The narrative manner of these romances, which Chaucer must have learned both from hearing minstrels in London and Westminster and from reading books, especially anthologies such as the Auchinleck MS.,[12] formed an important part of his native poetic inheritance. He received it with mixed feelings; and these mixed feelings find expression in *Sir Thopas*. This remarkable piece is more than simply a burlesque on the hack-work of tail-rhymers such as Thomas Chestre, though it is that. In some respects it may stand as an image, or cartoon, of Ricardian poetry itself, representing many of the weaknesses and some of the strengths not merely of the hacks but also of the true poets of the age, including Chaucer himself. Stylistically, the poem represents what Chaucer and his contemporaries accepted, as well as what they rejected, of native traditions. It should, therefore, repay consideration in the present context.

The most obvious part of the joke in *Thopas* is that Geoffrey Chaucer should be capable, in the way of a tale on the road to Canterbury, of nothing better than this 'drasty' bit of tail-rhyme. Even if we do not agree with critics like E. T. Donaldson[13] who hold that the pilgrim Chaucer is represented as genuinely incapable of anything better and genuinely indignant at the Host's interruption, the facts remain that the pilgrim does not introduce his tale as a burlesque, and that Harry Bailey seems to speak for everyone when he says he has heard enough. Chaucer the pilgrim may not be as incapable as Donaldson thinks; but at least he wants to tease his companions into thinking him incapable. On either reading, tail-rhyme represents a most degraded form of narrative verse, the very opposite of the polished performance which we would have expected from the one poet on the pilgrimage. But when we come to compare *Thopas* in some detail with the rest of Chaucer's work, we begin to see that the familiar self-depreciating joke has a second stage to it. For the poem, where it is bad, is often bad in a strikingly

Chaucerian way. Certainly it does exhibit, as critics and editors have pointed out, many features (forms, words, rhymes, compounds, phrases, collocations) which are recorded nowhere else in Chaucer's work; and where these unique features figure in the hack-work of the age one may suspect that they are positively unChaucerian. In such cases we suppose, reasonably enough, that Chaucer, as a fastidious man of letters with a good ear for niceties of language, is enjoying a straightforward joke at the expense of Thomas Chestre and the rest.[14] But many other similar features, at which we laugh with equal readiness, prove on investigation to occur also in Chaucer's unparodic verse, and even to be characteristic of it. The parody in *Thopas*, as Dieter Mehl says in his book on the romances, 'often makes fun of conventions which Chaucer himself used at other times in all seriousness'.[15] The evidence of the concordance supports this conclusion. It suggests that the relationship between *Thopas* and the rest of Chaucer's work is more equivocal, and much more interesting, than appears at first sight.

The first stanza of the poem will provide sufficient illustration for present purposes:

> Listeth, lordes, in good entent,
> And I wol telle verrayment
> Of myrthe and of solas;
> Al of a knyght was fair and gent
> In bataille and in tourneyment,
> His name was sire Thopas.　　(vii. 712–17)

'Metre', wrote Coleridge, 'tends to increase the vivacity and susceptibility both of the general feelings and of the attention.'[16] In the present case, the bumpy non-Chaucerian metrical form – what the Host, when he interrupts, calls 'rym dogerel' – sets up and sustains in the reader an increased susceptibility to the ridiculous. Thus Chaucer's appeal for the attention of his listeners strikes us, despite the justification it derives from the circumstances of the pilgrimage, as naïve and stilted. The manner is that of a minstrel trying to capture the attention of listeners at a feast or in a tavern.[17] Yet Ruth Crosby has shown, in an important essay, that passages of direct address as if to a listening audience are common enough in Chaucer's own serious work, and that appeals for the attention of that audience are to be found, not only among the Canterbury pilgrims, but also in such poems as the *House of Fame* and *Troilus* where the narrator has no fictive occasion for them.[18] The most interesting of the specific parallels to the opening of *Thopas* occurs towards the beginning of *Troilus*, at the point where, after some ornate preliminaries, Chaucer turns to his story:

> Now herkneth with a good entencioun,
> For now wil I gon streght to my matere,
> In which ye may the double sorwes here
> Of Troilus in lovynge of Criseyde.   (i. 52–5)

The metre and movement of this are, of course, quite unlike the doggerel of *Thopas*. The diction is also much more elevated: Chaucer here uses 'herkneth' instead of the apparently low word 'list' (which he uses only in *Sir Thopas*),[19] avoids the vulgar form of address 'lordes', selects 'with a good entencioun' in place of the less dignified 'in good entent' (achieving a more sophisticated rhyme, with 'compassioun', in the process), and introduces the learned term 'matere'. Yet these differences, striking as they are, do not conceal the kinship between the two passages. At the beginning of his grandest work, Chaucer makes just the same appeal to his audience for their attention as he makes at the beginning of *Sir Thopas*, with the added assurance that he intends to waste no time: 'For now wil I gon *streght* to my matere'. Similar assurances are to be found elsewhere in *Troilus*:

> But al passe I, lest ye to longe dwelle;
> For for o fyn is al that evere I telle.   (ii. 1595–6)

In passages like these the poet accepts, though not without his famous smile (what is the 'o fyn'?), the humble role of minstrel-entertainer. It is hard to imagine Dante or that other 'lauriat poete' of Italy, Petrarch, condescending to such assurances and such appeals.

The narrator's appeal for the attention of his audience is supported, at the opening of *Sir Thopas* and afterwards, by what Mehl aptly describes as a 'salesman-like' manner.[20] This is to be a first-class occasion. The audience must listen attentively ('in good entent') while the entertainer tells truly ('verrayment') all about a knight who is everything that a knight should be. It would have been even more obvious to a contemporary reader than it is to us that Chaucer here makes fun of a poetry more naïve and popular than his own. 'In good entent' is used as a vaguely intensive fill-up for rhyme elsewhere in Chaucer's own work (for example in the *Legend of Good Women* 1149); but nowhere else does it rhyme without a final -*e*, as here with 'verrayment'. This is a touch of 'drasty rymyng' imitated from tail-rhyme poetry or some similar source. The word 'verrayment' itself occurs nowhere else in Chaucer, though the *O.E.D.* records it in many less fastidious writers of the fourteenth and fifteenth centuries, usually in rhyme. Again, the phrase 'fair and gent' introduces an epithet which Chaucer uses very rarely, and never, it would seem, without some ironic inflection.[21] Like 'verrayment', 'gent' lacks precision and force, especially in the present context which concerns Thopas's behaviour in battles and tournaments. Chaucer's burlesque seems here to have as its object that indiscriminate use of superlative and intensive language which we find in the romances, where the language of enthusiasm very soon became devalued and evacuated of its significance. There is another touch of this in the same line of *Thopas*:

> *Al* of a knyght was fair and gent.

This should mean that the narrator intends to tell his hero's whole story, as the Danish singer in *Beowulf* tells 'wel-hwylc . . . þæt he fram Sigemunde secgan hyrde'; but in contexts like these 'all' is little more than a rhythmic fill-up, tinged with the entertainer's enthusiasm for his subject. I cannot find examples of the usage elsewhere in Chaucer. It seems to belong to the popular romance and the ballad.[22]

Details apart, however, the intensive manner of *Thopas* does not strike the modern reader as fundamentally unChaucerian. Chaucer may not use the word 'verrayment' elsewhere, but he does, as Miss Crosby observes, use many other very similar asseverations.[23] Words such as 'certain', 'iwis', 'truly', 'doubtless', and phrases such as 'for sooth', 'without lie', 'sooth to tell', are part and parcel of Chaucer's staple manner. The encomiastic expressions are also highly characteristic of Chaucer's manner, though the particular word 'gent' is not. The General Prologue to the *Canterbury Tales* is a veritable *locus classicus* of sustained superlative. Each pilgrim seems to be supreme in his own kind: the Knight, 'a verray parfit gentil knyght'; the Monk, 'a manly man, to been an abbot able'; the Parson, 'a bettre preest I trowe that nowher noon ys'; the Summoner, 'a bettre felawe sholde men noght fynde' . . . but it is unnecessary to multiply examples of an extravagant manner which everyone will recognize. To some extent, no doubt, this manner may be explained by reference to French courtly poetry and the rhetorical Latin verse of the Schools; but the immediate stylistic effect in Chaucer is commonly simple and minstrelesque, even 'salesman-like'. Any reader of Dante or Milton will feel this strongly enough when he comes upon passages like the following in *Troilus*:

> The wrath, as I bigan yow for to seye,
> Of Troilus the Grekis boughten deere.
> For thousandes his hondes maden deye,
> As he that was withouten any peere,
> Save Ector, in his tyme, as I kan heere.
>
> (v. 1800–4)

Coming after the disarming simplicity of 'as I bigan yow for to seye', that 'thousandes' strikes a note of naïve extravagance not unworthy of *Sir Thopas*.[24]

Modern criticism inclines to the view that this naïve intensive note never sounds in Chaucer without a harmonic overtone of irony. The praise and the enthusiasm are always, according to this view, qualified either by the speaker himself or by our knowledge of him. Thus in the General Prologue the undiscriminating enthusiasm of the pilgrim Chaucer for his fellow guests at the Tabard is plainly inadequate, whether or not we choose to credit him with knowing it (a problem here, as in *Sir Thopas*); and his intensive language is therefore contained within a larger stylistic complex, a complex which lies quite beyond the attainments of minstrel poetry. Even in *Troilus*, many critics would argue, the narrator is himself a dramatic person such as might well make extravagant claims for his hero's prowess at a painful moment just before Achilles kills him.[25] Such ironic articulation of speech is indeed highly characteristic not only of Chaucer but also of the other Ricardian poets. It helps, as I shall argue later, to accommodate a rather limited and fundamentally simple inherited idiom to more complex and sophisticated purposes. But the point to notice here is just how vigorously the simple idiom does assert itself – more vigorously, in the passage from the end of *Troilus*, than any ironic overtones which we may, somewhat doubtfully in this place, credit to the sophisticated Chaucer.

The third kind of minstrel feature which can be illustrated from the opening of *Thopas*, besides address to the audience and superlative manner, is the use of stock phrases for purposes of metre and rhyme. The presence of such phrases in Chaucer's earlier work is clearly demonstrated in D. S. Brewer's comparison of what he rather generously calls the 'apparently slack style' of the opening of the *Book of the Duchess* with the 'sober, well-languaged' style of its French source, one of Froissart's poems.[26] Miss Crosby, furthermore, presents evidence to show that stock phrases belonging to 'the conventional language of poetry intended for oral recitation by the minstrel' are to be found throughout the whole range of Chaucer's work, as well in the later as in the earlier.[27] This conclusion will be accepted by anyone who has traced the stock phrases of *Thopas* in the Chaucer concordance. The third line of the opening stanza provides a relatively innocuous example: 'Of myrthe and of solas'. This coupling makes a small contribution to the *Thopas* joke; yet it has many parallels elsewhere in Chaucer's work:

> Hoom with his wyf he gooth to his contree,
> Nat fer fro Pedmark, ther his dwellyng was,
> Where as he lyveth in blisse and in solas.
>
> (*Canterbury Tales* v. 800–2)

Later in the same *Franklin's Tale*:

> And hoom they goon in joye and in solas.
>
> (*C.T.* v. 1019)

In the *Miller's Tale*:

> And thus lith Alison and Nicholas,
> In bisynesse of myrthe and of solas.
>
> (*C.T.* i. 3653–4)

These examples are enough to show that the coupling of the rhyme-word 'solas' with some synonymous noun (does it much matter which?) is admitted into Chaucer's graver, as well as his lighter, narrative style; and many other similar couplings could be found there. Miss Crosby, for example, cites fourteen examples of 'leef and dere', four (all in rhyme) in *Troilus*.[28] Another slightly different kind of coupling is illustrated in the next line of *Thopas*: 'Al of a knyght was fair and gent'. Here two epithets not synonymous but closely related in meaning make up a stock descriptive phrase. Similar phrases appear not infrequently in Chaucer's non-parodic verse, though often with an ironic twist. Two familiar examples from the General Prologue will illustrate this:

> A Sergeant of the Lawe, war and wys,
> That often hadde been at the Parvys.
>
> (*C.T.* i. 309–10)

And in a more Gallic manner:

> Ther was also a Nonne, a Prioresse,
> That of hir smylyng was ful symple and coy.[29]
>
> (*C.T.* i. 118–19)

This 'doublet style', as it has been called, takes more forms than can be illustrated from the specimen stanza – some of them highly characteristic, like the comprehensive alternative phrases, 'day ne nyght', 'cometh or gooth', 'joye or sorowe', discussed by Brewer.[30] But such phrases are, in any case, too insipid to bear extensive illustration.

Chaucer's dependence in *Sir Thopas* upon prefabricated phrases means, among other things, that his rhymes are very predictable. He makes a joke of this by breaking the tale off in the middle of a line which it is only too easy for the reader to complete for himself:

> 'Hymself drank water of the well,
> As dide the knyght sire Percyvell
>   So worly under wede,
> Til on a day – '
> 'Namoore of this, for Goddes dignitee,'
> Quod oure Hooste.   (*C.T.* vii. 915–20)

'Til on a day – '. The reader acquainted with the popular romances does not need the earlier line 'And so bifel upon a day' (748) for him to feel the phantom conclusion to Chaucer's amputated line: 'Til on a day it so bifel'. The rhyme is completely and ridiculously inevitable, as so often in the romances. Yet here once more *Thopas* proves to represent not only the art of doggerel rhymers but also, in caricature, Chaucer's own art. In his comparison between the rhyming techniques of Chaucer and Pope, W. K. Wimsatt stresses the greater 'cleverness' and unpredictability of rhyme achieved by the later poet.[31] Chaucer does have his own kinds of clever, difficult rhyme, such as the punning kind (*rime équivoque*) favoured by contemporary French art-poets:

The hooly blisful martir for to seke,
That hem hath holpen whan that they were seeke.[32]

(*C.T.* i. 17–18)

But the modern reader, who does not usually enjoy punning rhymes anyway, will be more struck by Chaucer's readiness, in comparison with later poets, to take easy rhymes from stock. There are many lines elsewhere in the *Canterbury Tales* just as easy to complete as the last line of *Thopas*.

The positive significance of *Sir Thopas* for a study of Chaucer's style might be summed up by saying that the poem represents the vigorous wild stock upon which were grafted Chaucer's other more literary and sophisticated styles – the lofty, singing, Renaissance style (as in some of the invocations and similes in *Troilus*); the obscure or alembicated style (as in the stanzas on Pedro the Cruel in the *Monk's Tale*); the rich, learned style (as in the opening of the second part of the *Squire's Tale*); the plain style of abbreviated narrative (as in the *Legend of Good Women*); the broad colloquial style (as in the Prologue to the *Manciple's Tale*); the 'Horatian' epistolary style of the *Envoy to Scogan*.[33] In general, these remarkable experiments represent, as D. S. Brewer says, 'Chaucer's progressive immersion in European literary culture'.[34] Some of them are of the first importance for the subsequent development of English poetry. C. S. Lewis was right when he said that a single line from *Anelida and Arcite*, 'Singest with vois memorial in the shade', seems to contain 'the germ of the whole central tradition of high poetical language in England'.[35] Yet such achievements, however great their historical importance and intrinsic value, lie too far off from the norms of Ricardian writing to require discussion here. They are not, in themselves, particularly characteristic either of the period or of its greatest representative. 'Singest with vois memorial in the shade' is not a specially Chaucerian line, taken out of context. The distinctive achievement lies in the 'grafting' of such things on to the wild stock.

The proem to the second book of the *House of Fame* illustrates this art of grafting:

> Now herkeneth, every maner man
> That Englissh understonde kan
> And listeth of my drem to lere.
> For now at erste shul ye here

So sely an avisyon,
That Isaye, ne Scipion,
Ne kyng Nabugodonosor,
Pharoo, Turnus, ne Elcanor,
Ne mette such a drem as this!
Now faire blisful, O Cipris,
So be my favour at this tyme!
And ye, me to endite and ryme
Helpeth, that on Parnaso duelle,
Be Elicon, the clere welle.
O Thought, that wrot al that I mette,
And in the tresorye hyt shette
Of my brayn, now shal men se
Yf any vertu in the be,
To tellen al my drem aryght.
Now kythe thyn engyn and myght!   (509–28)

The modern reader of a passage such as this cannot, and should not, fail to register a certain impression of old-fashioned simplicity. In the first part of this proem, especially, what I have been calling minstrel features are very evident: the appeal for the attention of the audience ('Now herkeneth . . .'), the 'salesman-like' manner ('so sely an avisyon') supported in this case by a typically indiscriminate list of precedents, the stock phrases ('listeth . . . to lere'), the fill-ups ('at erste') and the unclever rhymes ('lere . . . here'). Later in the passage, imitations of Italian art-poetry (chiefly Dante) in the three addresses, to Venus, the Muses and Thought, introduce stylistic features of quite a different kind.[36] In the address to the Muses, rhetorical periphrasis combines with abnormal word-order (inversion of verb and object, separation of pronoun from relative clause) to produce a 'difficult' effect reminiscent of Dante and Latin poetry. But the difficulty is not marked, for the diction remains simple (except in the phrase 'tresorye . . . of my brayn'); and the whole passage produces an effect more homogeneous than analysis of its parts might suggest. The tone modulates smoothly and easily from the frank minstrelsy of the opening address to the audience, through the modest appeal to Venus, on to the grander invocations of the Muses and Thought. In the context which this style creates, Dante and Thomas Chestre can exert their respective influences together without coming into conflict.[37]

22

This easy breadth of manner is quite unlike what one finds in the poetry of Machaut, or Boccaccio, or Petrarch. It reminds one rather of such poets as the Spaniard Juan Ruiz (first half of the fourteenth century). In Ruiz's *Libro de Buen Amor*, courtly, learned and demotic elements fuse to produce a style which has reminded several English critics of Chaucer. In his book on Spanish literature, Gerald Brenan speaks of 'that intensely human medieval democracy of which Spain and England, so far as literature is concerned, provide the best examples'.[38] Even those who are most sceptical of 'romantic fictions' about the Middle Ages might agree that such a democracy, if it had existed, would have produced something very like the kind of writing which we find in the *Libro de Buen Amor* and in the *House of Fame*.[39]

II

At the beginning of the first version of his *Confessio Amantis*, John Gower says that it is his intention to write a poem in English for King Richard because 'fewe men endite/ In oure englissh' (Prol. 22–3). Gower, as I shall suggest later, felt less sympathy for, and drew less upon, existing English poetry than did Chaucer; but no doubt even the latter, with his more catholic tastes, would have been obliged to agree that their predecessors in English poetry had left them no very distinguished precedents. Most of the 'lost literature of medieval England', after all, was lost as much to Chaucer and Gower as it is to us;[40] and much of what we do know (Anglo-Saxon poetry for example) they did not. Collections such as the Auchinleck MS., despite their great bulk, offered little work of sufficient distinction to command the respect of sophisticated London readers. If that was their native heritage (and where else are we to look for it?), then it was a poor thing – poorer by far than the inheritance of later English poets, and poorer even than that of some of their own English contemporaries.

Unlike Chaucer and Gower, the poets of the Alliterative Revival were heirs to a tradition which had in English a long and distinguished history, going right back to the bards or 'scops' of Anglo-Saxon times. Their alliterative line, unlike the tail-rhyme stanza or the octosyllabic couplet, had once enjoyed a classical age in England; and although the poetry of that classical age was no longer read, the metre still carried with it traditions of style, diction and syntax, sometimes of great antiquity, of which the 'maker' could feel proud.[41] None of the poets of the Auchinleck MS. would have spoken of his craft as does the author of *Winner and Waster*, an alliterative poem of the 1350s, in his prologue:

> Whylome were lordes in londe that loved in thaire hertis
> To here makers of myrthes, that matirs couthe fynde . . .
> Bot now a childe appon chere, withowttenn chyn-wedys,
> That never wroghte thurgh witt three wordes togedire,
> Fro he can jangle als a jaye, and japes can telle,
> He shall be levede and lovede and lett of a while
> Wele more than the man that makes hymselven.
> Bot never the lattere at the laste, when ledys bene knawen,
> Werke witnesse will bere who wirche kane beste. (20–1, 24–30)

Such complaints are always somewhat conventional; but one can sympathize with this author's feelings about the performances of unskilled and undignified literary entertainers. His art may be stiff and archaic, in this passage at least; but it is higher than the art of most of the Auchinleck poets. Though 'chyn-wedys' seems a rather absurd way of saying 'beard', the compound is a true latterday kenning, exhibiting the authentic riddling structure of Old English poetic expressions such as 'whale-road'.[42] It does, as the author claims, take wit to work these two words together, and it also takes a little wit to understand the result. The same cannot be said of 'fair and gent', 'myrthe and solas', and the rest.

Some decades after the writing of *Winner and Waster*, the author of *Sir Gawain and the Green Knight* expresses in his prologue a similar pride in the art of alliterative verse and its antiquity 'in londe':

> Forthi an aunter in erde I attle to schawe,
> That a selly in sight summe men hit holden,
> And an outtrage awenture of Arthurez wonderez.
> If ye wyl lysten this laye bot on littel quile,
> I schal telle hit as-tit, as I in toun herde,
> > with tonge,
> > As hit is stad and stoken
> > In stori stif and stronge,
> > With lel letteres loken,
> > In londe so hatz ben longe. (27–36)

The interpretation of the last part of this paragraph is a matter of dispute. I take the lines to mean that the story, in its present form, is 'fastened with true (i.e. correctly alliterating) letters, as has long been the custom in the land'.[43] Yet the poet, if he does indeed express pride in his ancient craft, also in the same passage exhibits features of style which belong to the newer, baser art of the 'geestour'. The characteristic relationship between minstrel and audience is established by the appeal for attention, coupled with assurances that the poem will be short – 'lest ye to longe dwelle', as Chaucer says in *Troilus*. At the end of his third fitt, the poet makes another such appeal more dramatically, on the eve of his hero's encounter at the Green Chapel:

> Let hym lyye there stille,
> He hatz nere that he soght;
> And ye wyl a whyle be stylle
> I schal telle yow how they wroght.   (1994–7)

Less artful addresses of the same kind are to be found elsewhere in the manuscript. In *Purity*:

> Yif ye wolde tyght me a tom, telle hit I wolde   (1153)

and in *Patience*:

> Wyl ye tary a lyttel tyne and tent me a whyle,
> I schal wysse yow ther-wyth as holy wryt telles.   (59–60)

These passages, each with its deferential 'If you will listen . . .', suggest a relation between poet and audience different from that prevailing in earlier times. Old English bards sing without apology or explanation, taking their audience's attention and interest for granted:

> Hwaet we Gar-Dena in gear-dagum
> þeod-cyninga þrym gefrunon.   (*Beowulf* 1–2)

The Middle English 'maker of myrthes', less formal and hieratic, apologizes, explains, asseverates, and generally tries in minstrel fashion to keep his audience happy.

This change in the relationship between poet and audience is associated with a marked decline of verbal artistry in the alliterative verse of the Middle English period. In general this verse is more monotonous, less subtle and rigorous, than Anglo-Saxon verse. The

passage quoted above from the *Gawain* poet's prologue provides a
typical illustration of this decline, in the lines:

> Forthi an aunter in erde I attle to schawe,
> That a selly in sight summe men hit holden.

In both these lines, the second alliterating syllable in the first half-
line (where, as against the more restrained and elegant usage of
classical Old English, both lifts usually alliterate in Middle English)
is achieved by the too easy use of a prepositional phrase: 'an aunter
in erde', 'a selly *in sight*'. The use of prepositional phrases in this
section of the line is a habit widespread among the poets of the
Alliterative Revival.[44] There are two objections to this habit. First,
it produces an effect of monotony, hard to illustrate in specimen
passages. The pair of occurrences cited might be justified on grounds
of parallel sense; but the sheer frequency of the phenomenon eventually defeats such explanations. In the short passage quoted from
Winner and Waster, we find 'lordes in londe', 'makers of myrthes',
and 'childe appon chere', not to mention '. . . thurgh witt' and
'. . . at the laste', all at the same point in the line. In a single stanza
of *Sir Gawain* itself (2212-33), fourteen lines out of twenty-two
achieve their second alliterating stave by the use of a prepositional
phrase.[45] The parallelisms of syntax which result from this and other
similar habits may be exploited for rhetorical effect; but they often
produce an effect of mere flatness and monotony. Alliterative verse
shows to better advantage when, as is consistently the case in the
best Anglo-Saxon poetry, the sense is '*variously* drawn out from one
verse into another'.

These prepositional phrases illustrate also the excessive tolerance
extended by Middle English alliterative poets to pleonasm, and
sometimes to sheer vacuity of expression. The *Gawain* poet's
phrase 'an aunter in erde' may, in the light of his previous references to Britain as the land of marvels, be understood as 'an adventure in *this* land'; but the prepositional adjunct seems more probably
a simple pleonasm, here as elsewhere in the same metrical position:

> Half etayn in erde I hope that he were   (140)

and:

> Alle of ermyn in erde, his hode of the same.   (881)

The phrase 'a selly in sight' is more unfortunate. When Arthur and his court are actually confronted with the Green Knight, later in the poem, the reader can accept even a double emphasis on sight:

> Such a fole upon folde, ne freke that hym rydes,
> Watz never sene in that sale wyth syght er that tyme,
>   with yye.[46]   (196–8)

But the same emphasis is inappropriate in the earlier context. The men who judge the Adventure of the Green Chapel to be marvellous must, as contemporaries of the poet, judge by ear rather than eye. 'A selly to here' is what this context demands; but that, of course, would reduce the alliterative locking of the two half-lines.

In her most careful and sympathetic study of the style of *Sir Gawain*, Miss Borroff has presented the case for pleonastic phrases such as these.[47] She admits that they count as faults where they are 'obtrusive' or 'inappropriate', as I judge 'in sight' to be; but otherwise she is inclined to defend their use. She says: 'The pleonasm as a legitimate device of elevated style produces effects of emphasis and retardation of pace because of its tautological character.' Of lines 196–8, quoted above, she writes: 'The retardation of narrative pace produced by *upon folde, wyth syght,* and *with yye,* together with the emphasis upon "seeing", enhance the description of the suspended activity, the virtual stupefaction, produced by the spectacle of the Green Knight on his green horse.' But what if 'wyth syght' and 'with yye' did not contribute to the appropriate 'emphasis upon "seeing"'? What if they were truly pleonastic? Could we then allow the poet to retard the pace of his narrative, however expressively, by their use? Poets who adopt such a relatively undemanding metre as the Middle English alliterative line are under a special obligation, surely, to respect the other demands of sense and context. Otherwise they create an unpleasantly facile effect. The *Gawain* poet is certainly not one of those 'that never wroghte thurgh witt three wordes togedire'. Indeed, he is generally and rightly held to be the most technically proficient of all the poets of the Revival.[48] Yet even his 'working of words together' suffers by comparison with that found in the best of Old English poetry. The complex formulaic techniques of the *Beowulf* poet rarely create that effect of stylistic facility which is so common a fault in the poems of the Revival.

A comparison between *Beowulf* and *Gawain*, the best with the best, would reveal many features of style which the later poet shares not with his eighth-century predecessor but with his fourteenth-century contemporaries, and even with *Sir Thopas*. Concerning the *Gawain* poet's use of what she calls 'qualitative adjectives', Miss Borroff writes: 'In general these adjectives serve to intensify; referring to the persons and scenes viewed sympathetically by the narrator, they impute qualities of moral excellence and material splendour; referring to hardships or dangers with which the heroes are confronted, they impute qualities of dreadfulness, fierceness, and strangeness.'[49] Such adjectives are used very frequently by the *Gawain* poet. Of the 'sympathetic' ones, 'rich', 'dear', 'bright', 'clean' and 'fair' each appears more than fifty times in the poems commonly attributed to him.[50] Miss Borroff is right when she says that 'the frequent use of adjectives such as these is . . . a traditional feature of the alliterative style'. Yet the effect which they create in *Gawain* or *Purity* is not the same as the effect created by the *Beowulf* poet with his corresponding epithets of praise, 'æþele', 'ærgod', 'wlonc', and the rest. It is nearer to the intensive manner of *Thopas* in being less formal, less measured, less discriminating. Compare, for example, the description of the giants before the Flood in *Purity*:

> Hit wern the fayrest of forme and of face als,
> The most and the myriest that maked wern ever,
> The styfest, the stalworthest that stod ever on fete,
> And lengest lyf in hem lent of ledez alle other. (253–6)

with the *Beowulf* poet's introduction of his hero:

> Þæt fram ham gefrægn Higelaces þegn,
> god mid Geatum, Grendles dæda;
> se wæs moncynnes mægenes strengest
> on þæm dæge þysses lifes,
> æþele ond eacen. (194–8)

The single superlative of the *Beowulf* poet, itself duly qualified ('the strongest at that time'), contrasts with the stream of superlatives in *Purity*. The Middle English poet lacks the discipline and weight of his great predecessor.

III

The Ricardian poets were born in an age when, as one critic puts it, 'the tradition of verbal art had been debased, and poets were often too easily satisfied'.[51] The verbal art of the poets of the Alliterative Revival cannot compare with that of the Old English scops any more than the art of the poets of the Auchinleck MS. can compare with that of the best French rhymers. In the circumstances, it is perhaps surprising that two such masters as Chaucer and the *Gawain* poet should have shown themselves so accommodating towards their respective English traditions. Each of them seems to take delight in the humblest traditional routines of his art. Even *Sir Thopas* expresses, in the bouncy rhythms and vigorous phrasing, its author's pleasure in those 'minstrel features' which are the objects of his ridicule. Like most good burlesque, it is a thoroughly genial piece of work.

The case is different with Gower and with Langland. *Piers Plowman* and *Confessio Amantis* have little enough in common so far as stylistic surface is concerned; but they stand in a similar relation to current English traditions of poetic art. Gower stands off from the traditions so generously represented in the work of Chaucer, just as Langland stands off from the traditions represented by the *Gawain* poet; and from this greater remoteness some similar consequences seem to follow, at least in the styles of the two poems.

Concerning Gower's style there exists a well-established, indeed an unchallenged, critical tradition. We have seen that Berthelette, in his edition of *Confessio Amantis* first printed in 1532, recommended Gower as a model of good English and a 'mooste plesunt and easy auctor'. By his use of the word 'easy' Berthelette seems to anticipate the later Augustan ideal of a style free from constraint or stiffness, smooth and without a trace of effort.[52] At any rate, the eighteenth-century reader did find much to admire in Gower. Thomas Warton wrote that 'by a critical cultivation of his native language, he laboured to reform its irregularities, and to establish an English style'.[53] Gower's nineteenth-century editor, Macaulay, praises him in similar terms:

> In the ease and naturalness of his movement within the fetters of the octosyllabic couplet he far surpasses his contemporaries, including Chaucer himself. Certain inversions of order and irregularities of construction he allows himself, and there are many stop-gaps of the conventional kind in the ordinary flow of his narrative; but in places where the matter requires it, his admirable management of the verse paragraph, the metrical

smoothness of his lines, attained without unnatural accent or forced order of words, and the neatness with which he expresses exactly what he has to say within the precise limits which he lays down for himself, show a finished mastery of expression which is surprising in that age of half-developed English style.[54]

In the present century, C. S. Lewis has written most eloquently in *The Allegory of Love* about Gower's 'plain style': 'He stands almost alone in the centuries before our Augustans in being a poet perfectly well bred.'[55]

Every reader of *Confessio Amantis* will recognize the felicity of Warton's phrase, 'a critical cultivation of his native language'. The results of this cultivation can be traced throughout the poem, in the story-telling manner of the Confessor, who speaks more correctly and fastidiously than Chaucer's pilgrims, as well as in the manner of his conversations with Amans.[56] The style is represented at its best in such a passage as the following, taken from one of the lover's confessions:

> And whan sche goth to hiere masse,
> That time schal noght overpasse,
> That I n'aproche hir ladihede,
> In aunter if I mai hire lede
> Unto the chapelle and ayein.
> Thanne is noght al mi weie in vein,
> Somdiel I mai the betre fare,
> Whan I, that mai noght fiele hir bare,
> Mai lede hire clothed in myn arm.   (iv. 1133–41)

The elegantly turned antithesis between 'bare' and 'clothed' in the last two lines releases all the sensuality latent in the word 'clothed', so that its very sound (as in Keats's 'wealth of *globed* peonies') becomes luxurious. One feels the touch of the lady on the lover's arm. To achieve such an effect without metaphor and without disturbing the continuity of the 'easy' or 'plain' style of the passage as a whole shows great mastery of the art of writing.

Yet Gower's style, though it represents a remarkable achievement, is not as good as some accounts suggest. Many readers who are persuaded by Lewis's advocacy to read *Confessio Amantis* find it, let us admit, disappointing. No long poem, of course, can be expected to sustain the level of those choice passages which critics quote; but the fact remains that Gower's plain style is often not so much plain as threadbare. The 'metrical smoothness' of which Macaulay speaks is sustained with astonishing consistency, and there are many moments of great beauty; but the staple style is always dangerously close to sheer hebetude and dullness. Occasionally we are aroused by a certain Ricardian robustness in the narrative, as in the minstrelish opening of the frame-story:

> Upon the point that is befalle
> Of love, in which that I am falle,
> I thenke telle my matiere:
> Now herkne, who that wol it hiere,
> Of my fortune how that it ferde.
> This enderday, as I forthferde
> To walke, as I yow telle may . . .   (i. 93–9)

This passage is none the worse for being easily convertible (like so much of the more popular octosyllabic couplet verse of the period) into tail-rhyme:

> Upon the point that is befalle
> Of love, in which that I am falle,
>   As it is Goddes grace,
> I thenke telle my matiere:
> Now herkne, who that wol it hiere,
>   Al sittende in this place,
> Of my fortune how that it ferde.
> This enderday, as I forthferde
>   Miselven to solace . . .[57]

But in general Gower exercises his 'critical cultivation of his native language' at the expense of those elements (words like 'enderday',[58] phrases like 'as I yow telle may') which make such a conversion possible. The result of this selectivity is an undoubted gain in correctness and good breeding, but a loss in liveliness and energy. *Confessio Amantis* might be more widely read and admired today had Gower been less fastidious. One feels that in English his 'Augustanism' was somehow premature – though it already had precedents in French – and that his poem suffers a certain general lowering of vitality because of this. It is as if the English language was not yet rich enough to support the sacrifices which an exclusive doctrine of correctness demands. Gower's example shows how much Chaucer gained by his greater readiness to come to terms with what *Sir Thopas* stands for. *Confessio Amantis* is a much more remarkable poem than most imagine; but it does not have the centaur-like strength of the *Canterbury Tales*.

Like Gower, Langland exhibits a considerable degree of alienation from current English poetic traditions; but it is a different kind of alienation, reflecting the very different character and circumstances of Gower's fellow-citizen. The difference may conveniently be illustrated by comparing their habits of revision, for both poets were inveterate revisers of their work. In the case of *Confessio Amantis*, the numerous manuscripts of which exhibit (according to Macaulay) two major revisions of the original version, Gower seems to have been inspired to rewrite most often by a desire for greater elegance or correctness of metre and expression.[59] At the same time, the manuscripts show signs of authorial supervision even over such details as the capitalization of words.[60] As Macaulay says: 'We feel that we have to do with a literary craftsman who by laborious training has acquired an almost perfect mastery over his tools.'[61] Comparison of the three versions of *Piers Plowman* creates a different impression. Langland plainly had no scriptorium over which he could exercise the kind of supervisory vigilance which Gower seems to have exercised over the scribes of St Mary Overeys in Southwark.[62] Even Langland's own copies of his poem – the copies from which he worked in the process of revision – were apparently marred by many scribal errors.[63] In these circumstances, 'critical cultivation of his native language' might well have seemed to him rather a waste of time, since many of his finer points of usage would simply have got lost in the process of copying.[64] But in any case one suspects that Langland was not the man to care as Gower did about finer points of usage. In the absence of sound modern texts of the B- and C-versions of *Piers* to set beside Kane's A-text it is dangerous to commit oneself about Langland's revisions, especially where matters of verbal detail are concerned; but I doubt whether even the most careful editing will remove the impression that Langland was, in general, more concerned with what he said – what he had said in the earlier version, and what he wanted to say now – than with how he said it.

Yet Langland does develop his own brand of 'plain style', and this is based, something like Gower's, on the exclusion of traditional poetic expressions – in this case, the special diction and formulaic phraseology of the Alliterative Revival. The causes of this style lie, I believe, in the very nature of Langland's enterprise when he set out to compose in alliterative metre a poem such as *Piers*. Although, as I shall suggest in the next chapter, *Piers* manages to contain a surprising amount of sheer story-telling, it is still much further than a poem like *Sir Gawain* from established norms of alliterative verse-narrative. Considered as a poem of satire and complaint, the poem does have some precedents in the alliterative tradition – *Winner and Waster*, most notably, and also rhymed poems with heavy alliteration such as 'The Simonie' in the Auchinleck MS.[65] – but the tradition as a whole was not adapted to such purposes, any more than it was adapted to express the truths of the Christian religion. Thus, discussions of subjects such as the venality of judges or the salvation of the righteous heathen simply did not lend themselves to expression in stock alliterative terms as readily as did the description of a battle or a journey. However, it was possible, as the *Gawain* poet himself shows in many passages, to handle such subjects in a style considerably less untraditional than Langland's – witness the paraphrase of the Beatitudes in *Patience*, or the pentangle passage in *Sir Gawain*. Deeper reasons for Langland's way of writing may lie in the nature of the audience for which he wrote.[66] Most literary historians suppose that *Sir Gawain* was composed to be read aloud in the household of some magnate; and the nature of the poem seems to support this hypothesis. The poet speaks directly to an audience whose knowledge of alliterative diction he seems to be able to take for granted. No doubt the members of this audience were less well-versed in poetic lore than their Anglo-Saxon predecessors; but they were much better equipped to appreciate alliterative verse than most of the readers for whom Langland composed *Piers Plowman*. The evidence suggests that Langland worked for a general audience of clerks and pious, educated laymen, and that his poem very soon reached these people in many different parts of England. It would be a matter of chance whether such readers happened to be acquainted with alliterative traditions. Alliteration itself, of course, was and always had been a universal feature of expressive English; but the alliterative metre, with its closely associated traditions of diction and formula, was much better known in some parts of the country (especially the North and West) than in others.[67] So no alliterative poem directed at an indeterminate, national audience could afford to make more than the minimum of special demands upon the sympathy and understanding of its readers. What delighted a courtly audience in Cheshire might puzzle and irritate a studious rector in Lincolnshire.

However this may be, the evidence collected by J. P. Oakden shows that Langland makes quite exceptionally sparing use of the special diction of alliterative verse.[68] When he does use stock expressions, furthermore, he commonly turns them to oblique and ironic effect, as in the passage at the beginning of B Passus iii where Lady Mede is received by the King at Westminster:

> Curteysliche the clerke thanne, as the Kyng hight,
> Toke Mede bi the middel and broughte hir into chaumbre,
> And there was myrthe and mynstralcye Mede to plese.
> They that wonyeth in Westmynstre worschiped hir alle;
> Gentelliche with joye the justices somme
> Busked hem to the boure there the birde dwelled,
> To conforte hire kyndely by clergise leve. (iii. 9–15)

Here for once Langland is treating a topic common in alliterative verse of the traditional kind – the reception of a guest by a great household, as Sir Gawain is received at Hautdesert. He treats it, accordingly, in a style more richly conventional than is usual in his work. One notices the piling up of intensive adverbs, 'curteysliche', 'gentelliche', 'kyndely'; the poetical word 'birde', meaning 'damsel'; and the couplings 'myrthe and mynstralcye' and 'busked hem to the boure', both of which are formulaic.[69] Yet each of these poeticisms creates in this context an ironic effect. Mede is not what is usually meant by a 'birde'; the courtesy and kindness of the clerks and justices of Westminster is of a mercenary character; and the 'myrthe and mynstralcye' is inspired not by a courtly love of festivity but by the prospect of profit. An extraordinary number of the poeticisms in Langland's work are applied in this way, as if within marks of quotation, to unworthy subjects. Thus in Passus xiii the gluttonous friar is said to be 'as rody as a rose' (99) not because he is beautiful but because he is flushed with too much food and drink.[70] Later in the same passus, several superlative expressions of traditional poetic form are applied, in a kind of tirade, to a proud man:

> Wilnyng that men wende his witte were the best,
> Or for his crafty kunnynge, or of clerkes the wisest,

34

Or strengest on stede, or styvest under gurdel,
And lovelokest to loken on, and lelest of werkes.[71]

(xiii. 292-5)

It is characteristic of Langland that the full-blown formula 'styvest under gurdel' should occur (with a hint of sexual *double entendre* in 'stiff'?) only in this degraded context in his poem. He was hardly capable of using such expressions other than ironically.

This kind of ironical detachment appeals more to some readers than the 'full devout courage' with which the *Gawain* poet often uses similar formulas. But there can be no doubt that Langland, like Gower, pays a price for his alienation from current English poetic traditions. Langland is the only one of our four poets capable of sustained grandeur and sublimity of utterance; yet he is also the poet who, when he falls, falls lowest. Perhaps if he had been in a position to submit more to the traditional disciplines of the alliterative poet, he might have commanded a style richer and in its fashion more correct, without sacrificing the toughness and flexibility of line which are among his special achievements.

IV

Langland's ironic use of the diction of alliterative poetry is typical of the stratagems by which Ricardian poets accommodated to their own purposes the vigorous but relatively unsophisticated literary English of their day. Their characteristic mode of utterance is a kind of oblique simplicity. Unlike the poets of some later periods whose utterances look more complicated and interesting in isolation than they do in context, the Ricardian writers cultivate a manner in which, at its best, the simplicity of the individual utterance is the measure of its dependence upon a complex and interesting context. The context will have the effect of redirecting the utterance, as it were, and justifying its simplicity, as the context of the *Canterbury Tales* redirects and justifies what would otherwise be mere 'drasty rhyming' in *Sir Thopas*. In this section I want to look at some of these stratagems and accommodations in rather more detail.

The boldest and most effective of the stratagems is Chaucer's device of the Canterbury pilgrimage, by which all the tales which make up the bulk of the work are attributed to pilgrim-narrators. Such framing of tales has not, on the whole, been very successful in modern times; but it works well in the *Canterbury Tales*. This success is largely a matter of style; and it may be explained, in part, as follows. Chaucer was an intensely bookish poet, and in his metropolitan circles the new age of widespread literacy and the mass-production of books had already dawned.[72] In his *Canterbury Tales*, accordingly, the older face-to-face relationship between narrator and audience, the relationship characteristic of an age when books were scarce, is internalized and fictionalized; and the corresponding features of style are thus accommodated and given a new justification within the poem's fiction, to which in turn they lend strength and authenticity. Not only in the burlesque of *Thopas*, but in the other verse tales also, Chaucer exploits the vigorous manner of the minstrels and their frank way with an audience in order to achieve a lively representation of the pilgrims telling their stories on the Canterbury road:

> 'Now herkneth,' quod the Millere, 'alle and some! . .
> For I wol telle a legende and a lyf
> Bothe of a carpenter and of his wyf.'   (i. 3136, 3141–2)

The Knight is equally direct:

> Now wol I stynten of the goddes above,
> Of Mars, and of Venus, goddesse of love,
> And telle yow as pleynly as I kan
> The grete effect, for which that I bygan.   (i. 2479–82)

Chaucer did not have to invent this face-to-face story-telling manner. It is convincing, as no merely invented manner can be, because minstrel poetry was still in his day a living reality. What Chaucer the man of letters did invent was the perfectly-judged fiction of the pilgrimage. It is characteristic of both poets that whereas Gower's frame-story of the lover's private confession to the priest Genius establishes a context unfavourable to the broader kinds of minstrel effect,[73] Chaucer's frame-story positively encourages them. The same expressions which would seem out of place in the quiet tête-à-tête between Amans and Genius are just right for the circumstances of the pilgrim cavalcade: ' "Now herkneth," quod the Millere, "alle and some!" '

Langland cannot match the consummate artistry of Chaucer; but he does achieve in *Piers Plowman* a fictional form which is almost as felicitous, from the point of view of the stylistic constitution of the work, as the fictional form of the *Canterbury Tales*. I refer to his device of attributing most of the poem's expository utterances to certain allegorical persons who act as instructors to the dreamer Will. It may be that a straight, unfictional poem of exposition was impossible to achieve in the English of Langland's time. There existed, of course, many versified explanations of the Creed, the Pater Noster and other similar subjects at that time; but such simple, non-literary works of pastoral instruction offered no real precedent for true poets. A poet might choose to write in Latin; but if he chose the vernacular, he could hardly address his subject directly. Pope's English, the language of Locke and Berkeley, was adequate to express anything he might want to say about Man; but Langland's English, so far as concerned the expression of religious or philosophical ideas, was chiefly fashioned not by Ockham or Bradwardine but by the preachers. Owst has shown that Langland owed much to the preachers;[74] but their legacy was not an unmixed blessing. The preachers' idiom, especially when set to alliterative two-stress rhythms, is more remarkable for vigour than for subtlety and finesse. Yet Langland had a mind for subtlety as well as vigour; and he succeeds in accommodating, and to some degree transcending, the idiom of the preachers by building preachers into his poem, rather as Chaucer builds story-tellers into his.

A famous passage from the B-text will illustrate this:

For Trewthe telleth that love is triacle of hevene;
May no synne be on him sene that useth that spise,
And alle his werkes he wroughte with love as him liste;
And lered it Moises for the levest thing and moste like to hevene,
And also the plente of pees, moste precious of vertues.
For hevene myghte noughte holden it, it was so hevy of hymself,
Tyl it hadde of the erthe yeten his fylle,
And whan it haved of this folde flesshe and blode taken,
Was nevere leef upon lynde lighter therafter,
And portatyf and persant as the poynt of a nedle,
That myghte non armure it lette, ne non heigh walles. (i. 146–56)

If Langland had intended these lines to form a separate short unframed moral poem, like Chaucer's *Truth*, he probably would not have written them differently; yet their context in the longer poem, where they form part of Holy Church's instruction of Will, controls

and as it were hedges their style in a very special way. Holy Church
has begun this particular speech with a reproof to Will:

> 'Thow doted daffe,' quod she, 'dulle arne thi wittes;
> To litel latyn thow lernedest, lede, in thy youthe . . .
> It is a kynde knowyng,' quod he, 'that kenneth in thine herte
> For to lovye thi lorde . . .'   (i. 138–41)

In Will's dream, Holy Church is explaining about *caritas* to a
listener who is dull of wit and knows little Latin. This situation is
one version of the *magister* and *discipulus* convention which is found
in expository writing of all ages; but the relationship between the
situation and the style of the present passage is much more intimate
than in, say, Boethius's *De Consolatione Philosophiae*, where Philo-
sophia sets out to instruct Boethius. The extraordinary concreteness
and homeliness of the imagery both promotes the fiction and derives
justification from it. This, we surely feel, is just how an instructor
would appeal to such a listener, through his natural understanding
('kynde knowyng') of the processes of healing, eating, piercing. In
this way Langland, consciously or not, makes a virtue of the neces-
sities of his maternal tongue.

Holy Church is the first of a long line of Will's instructors in *Piers
Plowman*, especially in the *Vita* – Thought, Wit, Study, Clergy,
Scripture, Trajan, Imaginative, Anima, Liberum Arbitrium, Conscience. But a still more comprehensive framing device is represented by the figure of Will himself, the dreamer-narrator. The
presence of a narrator inside the poem's fictional world is a very
common feature of Ricardian work. In dream-poems proper, there
is the dreamer – in *Piers Plowman*, *Pearl*, the *Book of the Duchess*,
the *House of Fame*, the *Parliament of Fowls* and the G-version of
the *Legend of Good Women*. In pseudo-dream-poems, there is
the pseudo-dreamer – in *Confessio Amantis* and the F-version of
Chaucer's *Legend*. In the *Canterbury Tales*, which in this respect
represents a development out of the dream-poems, there is Chaucer
the pilgrim.[75] Such figures do not necessarily, so far as style is concerned, have any special significance. The 'Dante' who reports his
journey through the regions of the dead plays little part in the stylistic constitution of the *Divine Comedy*. It is hardly possible to distinguish his voice from the powerful and very personal idiom of the
author himself, nor does the poem encourage one to do so. In all the
English poems mentioned, the narrator does represent the author,

and in some cases *(Piers, House of Fame, Confessio Amantis, Canterbury Tales)* bears his name;[76] but the representation is less adequate here, for the English poets limit the perceptions of their narrators much more strictly than Dante does. Langland's Will, as we have seen, is accused of dull-wittedness and ignorance; and similar inadequacies are confessed by Gower's Amans:

> I am so rude in my degree
> And ek mi wittes ben so dulle,
> That I ne mai noght to the fulle
> Atteigne to so hih a lore.   (iv. 946–9)

The dreamer in *Pearl* and Chaucer's dreamers exhibit deficiencies of much the same kind.

The fact that a Ricardian poem represents itself as the report of a fictional narrator has never, so far as I know, persuaded an editor to print it wholly within marks of quotation; nor is it easy for the reader of, say, the *Knight's Tale* to bear steadily in mind that he is reading one pilgrim's report of another pilgrim's story. Yet the assigning of the *Canterbury Tales*, or *Piers Plowman*, as a complete utterance to a 'dull' and 'rude' source, Will or Geoffrey, does have consequences, though of the most general kind, for the stylistic constitution of these works. It means that the poet is not, in the last resort, directly committed to his work, as we feel Dante to be. He reserves for himself, as it were, the right to say 'But that is Will (or Geoffrey) speaking, not me'. More positively, it leaves the poet free to exploit possibilities in the contemporary vernacular which he might otherwise have found it difficult, as an educated man acquainted with politer languages, to come to terms with. The case of *Sir Thopas* makes it possible to suggest that Chaucer may have been aware of this. No doubt Langland was a less self-conscious and critical artist than Chaucer; but his results are almost as good. How well, after all, the figure of Will *works* in Langland's poem, and how much in the style of the poem he accommodates.

The fictionalized narrator also provides within these dream-poems and derivatives from dream-poems the chief means by which Ricardian poets articulate their own kind of irony. The term *eiron* in Aristotle's *Ethics* means a self-depreciating man; and its derivative *irony*, as Northrop Frye says, 'indicates a technique of appearing to be less than one is'.[77] Irony in this sense is highly characteristic of the Ricardian poet. It is not confined to those cases where the author has a dull representative within the fictional world of his poem. We find it also in straight narrative pieces which owe nothing, in this respect, to the techniques of dream-poetry. In *Troilus* Chaucer makes no attempt to smuggle a narrator into Troy; but he dramatizes his own relationship with the old love-story which he is telling, in such a way that he creates an image of himself as narrator which belongs unmistakably, together with that of Chaucer the pilgrim in the *Canterbury Tales*, to the tradition begun by the 'mazed' dreamer in the *Book of the Duchess*.[78] He is doing his best; he has no personal experience of love to draw on; so he will follow his authorities as closely as he can:

> Wherfore I nyl have neither thank ne blame
> Of al this werk, but prey yow mekely,
> Disblameth me, if any word be lame,
> For as myn auctour seyde, so sey I.
> Ek though I speeke of love unfelyngly,
> No wondre is, for it nothyng of newe is;
> A blynd man kan nat juggen wel in hewis.

(*Troilus* ii. 15–21)

Medieval rhetoricians commonly prescribe such passages of self-depreciation as a way of winning the goodwill of an audience; and the trick is too common in both medieval and Renaissance writing to count as distinctive, in itself, of any particular period. But the self-depreciation of Ricardian poets (especially Chaucer) is more significant stylistically than that of, say, Chrétien de Troyes or Edmund Spenser, because it is closely associated with a persistent verbal irony whereby simple, 'lame' and conventional expressions – expressions of the kind we have been prepared to accept from the narrator – prove to be charged with subtle and often damaging implications for which the author seems hardly to be responsible: 'Disblameth me . . .'.

Very often in such cases the narrator's voice, acting as the ostensible voice in a two-voiced ironic utterance, will employ some familiar turns of expression which carry clear points of social or moral criticism. We have already noticed examples of such two-part inventions in Chaucer's *Thopas* and in Langland's description of the reception of Lady Mede at Westminster. A further example may be taken from *Patience*, the version of the story of Jonah made, very probably, by the *Gawain* poet. The poet is describing Jonah's delight in the woodbine which God has sent to shelter him from the sun:

> The gome glyght on the grene graciouse leves,
> That ever wayved a wynde so wythe and so cole;
> The schyre sunne hit umbe-schon, thagh no shafte myght
> The mountance of a lyttel mote upon that man schyne.

> Thenne watz the gome so glad of his gay logge,
> Lys loltrande ther-inne lokande to toune;
> So blythe of his wod-bynde he balteres ther-under.   (453–9)

The intensifying manner of alliterative verse is represented in this passage by the enthusiastic epithets ('the grene graciouse leves', 'the schyre sunne', 'his gay logge'), the vividly emphatic claim that there was not enough sunbeam under the leaves to light up a single particle ('mote') of dust, and the two pairs of repeated 'so's' ('so wythe and so cole', 'so glad . . . so blythe'). But the enthusiasm is built up only to be undercut when God destroys the woodbine to teach Jonah a lesson; and this turns the extravagant idiom towards irony at Jonah's expense.

In the *Gawain* poet's treatment of Jonah, as in Langland's treatment of Lady Mede, the poet's intention is unmistakable: Jonah and Mede are each 'placed' by a mocking use of conventional poetic language. But in other places one finds a more equivocal effect. The poet appears to use conventional language not altogether straight, yet without articulating any clear ironic point. The language seems to be leaning over towards irony almost of its own accord. Examples of this kind of questionable irony occur in *Sir Gawain*. The poet's sense of people's inability to live up to their highest ideals gives rise, in this poem as in *Patience*, to many unmistakable ironic effects.[79] Yet there are other places where his intentions are much more difficult to read:

> This kyng lay at Camylot upon Krystmasse
> With mony luflych lorde, ledez of the best,
> Rekenly of the Rounde Table alle tho rich brether,
> With rych revel oryght and rechles merthes.
> Ther tournayed tulkes by tymes ful mony,
> Justed ful jolilé thise gentyle knightes.   (37–42)

Readers and critics have failed to agree in their responses to this passage, and understandably so. It does not look quite like a straight piece of romantic description. The piling-up of intensive language suggests, in this context, the possibility of something less than wholehearted enthusiasm. One notices especially the repetition of 'rich' in two successive phrases. Yet the passage is by no means clearly ironical, like the description of Jonah's response to his bush. Nor can we trace in it with any confidence a delicate blend of enthusiasm and irony. The poet seems content to create a vaguely equivocal effect by working the traditional alliterative style, without attempting to render precisely in the verse the mixed feelings about Arthur's court which the poem as a whole implies. Much the same might be said of the poet's handling of his hero Sir Gawain during the period of his fall from grace, between the moment of his concealment of the girdle and the moment of his confession to the Green Knight. There is – there must be! – irony in the application of eulogistic epithets to Gawain during this discreditable period (unless ironies are to be sought with still greater difficulty in the later descriptions of his remorse). Yet the actual effect in each particular case (e.g. 'Sir Gawayn the gode' 1926, 'the gentyle knyght' 2185) remains uncertain. The truth is that it sometimes takes an act of faith to find in the verbal detail of *Sir Gawain* the full subtlety and delicacy of mind which the general conception of the poem so unmistakably implies. In such cases the poet seems to be ill-served by his medium; and one is led to reflect upon the sacrifices forced on Ricardian poets, for all their stratagems and accommodations, by their decision to write English rather than French or Latin poetry.

V

The four Ricardian poets here under discussion are writers of strong individuality. Each one is an original. Despite the absence of biography and supporting anecdote, the distinctive personality of each stamps itself upon the reader's mind – immediately in the case of Chaucer and Langland, less immediately but no less firmly in the case of Gower and the *Gawain* poet. Each writes in his own unmistakable fashion: it is hard to imagine any serious difficulties of attribution arising between them. As we have seen, however, the relation of these very individual talents to the common traditions of English poetry in their day is such that their styles can usefully be compared. They share certain general strengths and weaknesses, which it is the purpose of this last section to assess.

By comparison with most later English poetry the work of all four Ricardian poets exhibits a loose-woven, open texture. Memorable passages and memorable episodes are more characteristic of these poets than memorable lines or phrases. Indeed, it seems to be against the particular nature of this poetry to remember it by felicities of word. A line such as 'Wrothe wynde of the welkyn wrastelez with the sunne', from the *Gawain* poet's description of the passing seasons, offers itself as a free-standing, eminently quotable description of a stormy autumn day. But the poet conceived the 'wrestling' of the wind (representative of autumn) with the sun (representative of summer) as it were abstractly, as part of a general conception of the 'threpe' or struggle (cf. l. 504) between each season and its appointed successor. The Van-Gogh-like, even Surrealistic, character which the image displays when we remember it out of context as direct physical description of the tumult of a stormy day is not necessarily beyond the range of this poet's calculations; but it is not, as would appear in a dictionary of quotations, the main point of the line. No doubt single lines and phrases of poetry always, or nearly always, undergo some degree of change and distortion when they are remembered out of context; but lines and phrases of Ricardian poetry seem particularly ill-adapted to survive under these conditions. Even the most striking of them (and comparatively few are 'striking') prove to be shaped with special strictness according to the demands of a larger context.

This strict subordination of the local and concentrated effect to the demands of a larger context marks the style of Ricardian poetry as essentially a long-poem style. One can see this in the short poems of Chaucer, the *Envoy to Scogan* or *Truth*, where much careful and intelligent workmanship somehow fails to produce a fully memorable result. There is something a little mysterious about the failure of Chaucer's not inconsiderable body of short poems to make the expected impression; but one reason is surely that the verbal texture remains, despite special efforts on Chaucer's part to exclude 'verse tags' and 'fillers', too open and loose for poems of this magnitude.[80] What is lacking is just that fundamental harmony between the scale of the poem and the scale of the language which we feel to be achieved without effort in the longer poems both of Chaucer and of his contemporaries. Just as John Donne's habitual style, which seems right in short poems, seems overwrought in long poems such as the *Anniversaries*, so Chaucer's style seems right in long poems but underwrought in short ones.[81] The long Ricardian poem, like the short metaphysical one, achieves a harmony which might be expressed in Coleridgean terms: it proposes to itself such gratification from each component *part* as is compatible with delight from the *whole*.

It is the nature of a true long-poem style to admit a certain degree of necessary dullness in the component parts. As Chaucer says, 'men may overlade a ship or barge'. Yet it must be said that dullness is to the Ricardian poet what false wit is to the Jacobean, or pomposity to the Anglo-Saxon, or sentimental poeticism to the Victorian: it is his most characteristic vice of style. Some things in Chaucer are as unexpected and as right as anything in English poetry:

> He was, if I shal yeven hym his laude,
> A theef, and eek a somnour, and a baude.
>
> (*C.T.* iii. 1353–4)

But such felicities are not characteristic of Ricardian poetry as a whole. There are comparatively few places where the shock of the right word unexpected stamps a phrase or line on to the reader's memory. The Ricardian poet submits more docilely than most of his successors to the constraints of idiom, rhythm, rhyme and alliteration. *Sir Thopas*, with its insipidity of language and predictability of rhyme, represents him at his characteristic worst.

As *Sir Thopas* reminds us, however, the dullness may be deceptive insofar as there exists a gap between the ostensible voice (which may be attributed to a fictional narrator or instructor) and the true voice of the poet. By stratagems, the Ricardian poet is able to speak more subtly, if sometimes also more questionably, than his idiom might seem to allow. His pervasively ironic mode of address is a source of flexibility, strength and an almost precocious subtlety. Yet the pervasiveness of this irony also marks limitations. Sometimes the ironic inflexion seems merely automatic, as if it expressed nothing more than the writer's habitually uneasy sense of the difficulty of expressing himself with complete adequacy in his chosen medium. There are traces of this morbidly reflexive irony in Chaucer, as there are in Jane Austen. Furthermore, because the poet so rarely 'speaks out' in direct, unguarded utterance, passages of full-throated grandeur or pathos are uncommon in Ricardian verse.[82] Thomas Warton was not wrong when he said that Langland was capable of the sublime, witness the speech of Christ at the Harrowing of Hell:

> 'For I that am lorde of lyf love is my drynke,
> And for that drynke today I deyde upon erthe.
> I faughte so me threstes yet for mannes soule sake;
> May no drynke me moiste ne my thruste slake
> Tyl the vendage falle in the vale of Josephath
> That I drynke righte ripe must, *resureccio mortuorum*'.
>
> (xviii. 363–8)

Grandeur and high pathos are also found occasionally in the work of Langland's contemporaries, as in *Pearl*:

> 'O perle,' quod I, 'in perles pyght,
> Art thou my perle that I haf playned,
> Regretted by myn one on nyghte? . . .'   (241–3)

and in *Troilus and Criseyde*:

> Thow oon, and two, and thre, eterne on lyve,
> That regnest ay in thre, and two, and oon,
> Uncircumscript, and al maist circumscrive,
> Us from visible and invisible foon
> Defende . . .   (v. 1863–7)

But such passages represent high styles which are hardly characteristic of the period: rather they anticipate later ages of English poetry. To this extent, Matthew Arnold was right when he said that Chaucer lacked 'high poetic seriousness'. In Arnold's context, as one can see from his choice of 'touchstone' examples ('In la sua volontade è nostra pace' is one of them), 'seriousness' implies speaking straight, not obliquely, to some great matter.[83] Neither Chaucer nor his great contemporaries are often in this sense 'serious'. Their characteristic manner lies, to adopt a favourite phrase of the period, 'betwixt earnest and game'. This oblique and often humorous approach to great matters – God, sin, death – does impose undoubted limitations on the range of Ricardian poetry, however attractive it may be to post-Arnoldian taste.

We should not, in any case, exaggerate the degree of irony and sophisticated reserve in Ricardian poetic styles. By comparison with the minstrels, these poets are indeed latterday masters of ironic sophistication; but by comparison with many of their peers on the continent, they appear conservative, serious, even old-fashioned. Above all, their style preserves against the encroachments of irony and sophistication the virtue – cardinal for their purposes – of being an absolutely authentic story-telling style. In this respect they differ from a writer such as Ariosto. The ironic tone which pervades *Orlando Furioso* bears standing witness to Ariosto's sense of the gulf separating him from his artless minstrel predecessors, the *cantastorie*.[84] It differs from Ricardian irony in that it seems to embrace the very process of story-telling itself, so that the reader of *Orlando Furioso* is never allowed to decide whether Ariosto means him in any sense to believe in the characters and their adventures. Ariosto plays his part as story-teller brilliantly but somewhat non-committally. By comparison, the English poets commit themselves 'with full devout courage' to the business of telling stories or reporting the telling of stories. The reader of *Troilus and Criseyde* or *Sir Gawain and the Green Knight* never doubts that he is to take the story, as a story, 'seriously'.

The favourite irony of the Ricardian poets, then, does not impair the fitness of their open-textured, long-poem styles for the business of story-telling. Indeed it is this simple fitness which most distinguishes the work of Chaucer or the *Gawain* poet, stylistically, from the writings of their successors. They command robust and adaptable styles which enable them to handle descriptions, actions, and different kinds of dialogue with equal facility; whereas Spenser in the *Faerie Queene* or Milton in *Paradise Lost* cultivate highly-wrought styles which, whatever their merits, are surely too singular for the general purposes of narrative, like that of William Morris in a later age. Unlike these later writers, the Ricardian writers were still in touch with a living tradition of story-telling in verse; and they were therefore able to deploy styles which, though more delicate and artful than those of the minstrels, were not too delicate and artful.[85] They preserve the aboriginal virtue which is present in *Sir Thopas*, even at the moment when the Host breaks in:

> Hymself drank water of the well,
> As dide the knyght sire Percyvell
> So worly under wede,
> Til on a day –

Chapter two

Ricardian Narrative

I

Neither lyric nor dramatic poetry can claim any prominent place in our picture of Ricardian poetry. Middle English plays and lyrics survive in considerable numbers, especially from the fourteenth and fifteenth centuries; but it is hard to distinguish in either corpus – uneven in quality, in each case, and mostly anonymous – anything substantial which can be assigned to a generation of writers flourishing between 1370 and 1400. There may have been a 'Ricardian lyric', even a 'Ricardian drama'; but their outlines cannot be traced in the surviving material. The religious lyrics in John of Grimestone's preaching-book (compiled about 1375), for example, have no distinguishable style of their own. According to Miss Woolf, they represent a period of transition, a 'divide', between two periods in the religious lyric; they 'repeat or recall the old style or show the beginnings of the new'.[1] Nor is this a great period in the history of the secular lyric. Gower says that Chaucer 'filled the land' with love-songs; but even Chaucer's lyrics, charming as they are, fail to amount to very much. No doubt many have been lost, however.

What does survive from the period is mostly not lyric or dramatic but narrative. This is certainly the case with the four poets under discussion here. *Troilus and Criseyde* and *Sir Gawain and the Green Knight*, *Canterbury Tales* and *Confessio Amantis*, *Patience* and *Purity*, *Pearl* and *Piers Plowman*: these are all – even *Piers* – eminently poems of narrative and description. The Ricardian poet deals in happenings – happenings which he has experienced or dreamed or read or learned about, or simply happenings. In this period of English poetry the voice of narrative prevails, as it does not in, say, the Jacobean period. Perhaps no subsequent period is so dominated by the narrative voice.

47

Love of story-telling is not characteristic of all late-medieval poets. The history of French poetry in the later Middle Ages shows a very marked movement away from story. In the twelfth and thirteenth centuries narrative verse flourished in France, witness the romances of Chrétien de Troyes and his imitators, or the many thirteenth-century *fabliaux*. But the thirteenth century also saw a growing taste for narrative in prose. H. J. Chaytor suggests two reasons: 'Readers began to discover that the action of a story moved more quickly in prose than in poetry and a demand for prose narratives began as the taste for individual reading increased.'[2] This growing demand was met by prose romances such as *Perlesvaus* (beginning of thirteenth century) and the Vulgate cycle of Arthurian romances (originally assembled 1215-30), and also by 'derhymed' versions of earlier verse romances such as the *Roman de Troie* of Benoît de Sainte-Maure. The work of the *dérimeurs* was taken up by continental patrons such as the Counts of Flanders.[3] By the middle of the fourteenth century, both the *fabliau* and the verse romance were out of fashion in France.[4] The typical long poem of this period is the *dit amoreux* ('amorous narrative'), a type stemming from the *Roman de la Rose*; and even that tradition had moved steadily away from story-telling in the century since Guillaume de Lorris. The story of Guillaume's allegory is relatively robust and well-developed. The persons and events of the garden of love in his poem have fictional body. In the work of his successors, allegory dwindles into a figure of speech and is subordinated increasingly to the soberly realistic, quasi-autobiographical account of some sentimental adventure.[5]

The resulting condition of French poetry in the 1360s, on the eve of our period, may be seen in the *Voir Dit* of Guillaume de Machaut (*c.* 1364) and in the *Espinette Amoureuse* (*c.* 1370) of Chaucer's contemporary and companion in the English court, Jean Froissart. The *Voir Dit*, as its title 'A True Tale' suggests, offers a basically realistic account of an affair between the elderly poet and a spirited young lady admirer. The comings and goings of Guillaume and Peronelle are described so circumstantially (with dates, places, transcripts of letters, references to contemporary persons, etc.) that one is tempted to suppose, with the poem's editor, that the piece is indeed 'true'.[6] If this is a mistake, at least the poet does much to encourage it. He has some allegory ('Dangier', 'Malebouche') and some classical *exempla* (Semiramis, Pyramus and Thisbe); but these are little more than decorative insets in the love-narrative. He also introduces ballades, rondels and other kinds of lyric. The poem, though much too long, is interesting; but it owes almost nothing to the story-telling impulse. The hero is a 'tenres homs', a tender man who shrinks from anything resembling an adventure;[7] and his little affair is almost wilfully uneventful. Much the same may be said of Froissart's account of a youthful love-adventure in the *Espinette Amoureuse*. Of this poem its editor writes: 'l'intrigue en demeure assez mince, le poète se bornant à nous conter par le menu les vicissitudes, qui n'ont rien de bouleversant – sauf pour lui –, de son premier amour.'[8] The *Espinette* shows very clearly how weak was the story-telling impulse in French verse at the beginning of our period. Like the *Voir Dit*, which Froissart admired, this poem employs allegory and *exemplum*, as well as lyric forms, for local decoration. But the main business of the poem lies in its quasi-autobiographical love-story, which is charming, tender and totally uneventful, like an essay by Leigh Hunt.[9]

Machaut and Froissart, like their contemporary Deschamps, devoted much of their poetic effort to the writing of lyric verse. Their achievement in the long narrative poem is fairly represented by the *Voir Dit* and the *Espinette*. Froissart did, it is true, compose a huge verse romance (30,771 lines) called *Méliador*, in which he attempted to add another branch to the Arthurian tree; but the attempt, according to those who have read the poem through, is a failure. Such a straight, traditional narrative poem seems to have been hardly viable in the France of the Valois.[10] Froissart's greatest achievement in narrative, of course, deals with 'true' contemporary events, and in prose – though we are told that he first thought of writing his Chronicles in verse, as Machaut had done in his little-read poem about Peter of Lusignan's capture of Alexandria, *Prise d'Alexandrie*.

Chaucer's early poem the *Book of the Duchess* (*c*. 1370) was deeply influenced by the *dits amoreux* of Machaut and Froissart.[11] But even here, in this very Gallic piece, we can detect that predilection for strong narrative which distinguishes English poets from French in this period. The story of Ceyx and Alcione in Chaucer's poem, for instance, is a great deal more vigorous and more prominent than are the classical *exempla* in Machaut. Later in Chaucer's career the difference of taste is more marked. In the Prologue to the *Legend of Good Women* Chaucer returns to the manner of the *dit amoreux*. The graceful little story of the poet's encounter with Cupid, with its superficial, decorative use of allegories (e.g. F. 160–3) and classical *exempla*, and its allusions to contemporary persons and circumstances, strongly recalls Machaut, as does the marvellous inset ballade 'Hyd, Absolon, thy gilte tresses clere'. But the Prologue differs from the customary French *dit* in that it serves to introduce a collection of stories – the 'legends' themselves which Alceste commands the poet to compose in honour of good women. Here, just as much as in the *Canterbury Tales*, Chaucer's work centres, in the English manner, on narrative.

In Gower's *Confessio Amantis* one can trace similar relationships between the Ricardian poet and his immediate predecessors and contemporaries in France. The *Confessio* owes a great deal not only (as has been generally recognized) to the *Roman de la Rose* but also to the later *dit amoreux*.[12] The story of unrequited love which Amans unfolds in the course of his confession to Genius is strongly reminiscent of the *Voir Dit*. Gower takes care, as Machaut does not, to dissociate himself from the lover-narrator; and he gives no names or dates or places. But his story of a man no longer young trying to win the affections of a beautiful woman is told in just the style of muted courtly realism which marks Machaut's poem. This story – 'qui n'a rien de bouleversant' – also pleases because it seems true, even though it is not. Gower's narrator, like Machaut's, speaks of love-service by war and adventure as something foreign to him (compare *Confessio* iv. 1615 ff. with *Voir Dit* 3507 ff.). He too is a 'tender', unadventurous, private kind of person – polite, but definitely not chivalrous. Like Machaut, too, Gower blends with his love-narrative some more or less discreet didacticism – 'courtois enseignemens', as Machaut calls it.[13] There is advice to a king in both poems, and also, more oddly, a list of discoverers and inventors. But although Gower comes closer than any of his contemporaries to Machaut's most fashionable manner, he also departs from it just as Chaucer does in the *Legend of Good Women*. The Lover's confession has much interest in its own right; but it also provides the occasion for all those stories which the Confessor tells in illustration of the Seven Deadly Sins. The confession is, in fact, a frame – though a broad and exquisitely decorated frame – for an encyclopaedic collection of stories. Again here Ricardian taste asserts itself against the sophisticated international Gothic taste which Machaut represents. Those *exempla* whose function in the *dit amoreux* is largely decorative become, in Gower's hands, the soul of the poem.

In the next generation of English poets, after 1400, the taste for 'voir dit' revives. The courtly, Chaucerian *Kingis Quair*, for example, represents itself as 'a longish narrative poem about love which is not allegorical, which is not even, like *Troilus,* a romance of lovers who lived long ago, but the literal story of a passion felt by the author for a real woman'.[14] The same taste appears, in non-courtly form, in the work of the most interesting of Chaucer's disciples, Thomas Hoccleve. In Hoccleve's so-called 'Series' of poems there are two well-managed narrative pieces, the *Tale of Jereslaus' Wife* and the *Tale of Jonathas,* both taken from the *Gesta Romanorum*; but these are overshadowed by the *Complaint* and the *Dialogue with a Friend.*[15] These autobiographical pieces convey so strong a sense of the sober, distressing realities of everyday life that they make the adventures from the *Gesta,* which they serve ostensibly to introduce, appear remote and fantastic. Hoccleve, he tells us, has had a mental breakdown, but he now feels capable once more of writing. The tales are what he writes: that is almost their only reality. Turning back from the 'Series' to Gower or Chaucer, one feels a different balance of forces. In the Canterbury pilgrimage Chaucer created his own kind of 'voir dit'; but even that representation of local and contemporary realities, strong and convincing as it is, fails to impair the other reality of the stories. Theseus exists in the *Knight's Tale* just as vigorously as does the Knight in the General Prologue and links.

One might guess, then, that English audiences in Richard's time were not particularly interested in the *verismo* of everyday contemporary life and love; and they certainly had not yet developed a taste for story-telling in prose – perhaps the first of English *dérimeurs* was Sir Thomas Malory. These audiences still retained an appetite for 'olde aproved storyes' told in verse: stories of Jewry (*Patience, Purity,* Gower's tale of Jephthah), of Troy (*Troilus,* Gower's tale of Paris and Helen), of Greece (the *Knight's Tale,* the story of Jason and Medea in Chaucer's *Legend of Good Women* and in Gower), of Rome (the *Physician's Tale,* Gower's tale of Mundus and Paulina), of Britain (the *Wife of Bath's Tale, Sir Gawain*). At the same time, the poets attempt a wide variety of narrative genres. They narrate far-flung adventures in the manner of the Greek romances, witness the tale of Constance told by both Chaucer and Gower, or Gower's concluding tale of Apollonius of Tyre; and also those equally fantastic 'merry tales' which French authors were no longer turning into *fabliaux*. They attempt animal fable, *exemplum*, saint's life, Breton lay – anything, one is tempted to say, with a story to it. Even *Piers Plowman*, though its design leaves little room for 'olde aproved storyes', exhibits much more gusto in narrative than does Deguileville's *Pèlerinage de Vie Humaine*, its equivalent in fourteenth-century France. One recalls the animal fable of the belling of the cat, the stories of Lady Mede and of the Pilgrimage to Truth, and, in the *Vita*, the story of Christ's joust in Jerusalem with its dramatic build-up in Passus xvi and xvii.

We shall have occasion later in this chapter to consider something of the subtle literary artistry displayed in Ricardian narrative verse; but it is necessary first to register its simpler qualities of sheer vigour and narrative conviction, qualities which it seems to owe very largely to earlier minstrel traditions. The Ricardian poets were more like men of letters than minstrels; but their literary sophistication is rarely exercised at the expense of the story. They preserve a pristine energy in their narrative, as few poets in the Renaissance or after have been able to do. In order to appreciate better these elusive qualities of 'energy' and 'conviction', we might turn for comparison to Italy, a country where, already in Chaucer's day, medieval narrative was giving way to Renaissance narrative, especially in the poetry of Boccaccio.

Italy in the fourteenth century still had a living tradition of story-telling in verse. Romances in *ottàva rima* were recited by minstrels in the piazzas of Tuscan cities. They were called *cantari*.[16] From these poems Boccaccio derived not only a metre but also many stylistic traits for his earliest poem, *Il Filostrato* (*c.* 1335), and also for his still more ambitious *Teseida* (*c.* 1340).[17] This derivation implies a commerce between the man of letters and the minstrel which recalls English (or Spanish) conditions rather than French. Yet a comparison between Boccaccio's poems and their English derivatives, *Troilus and Criseyde* and the *Knight's Tale*, shows clearly how the Italian pieces differ from English work.

In the remarkable Proem to *Il Filostrato*, Boccaccio makes the claim that he is writing, as Machaut or Froissart would have expressed it, 'de sentement'.[18] His poem springs, he says, out of his own experiences and personal feelings. It does not purport, like Machaut's *Voir Dit*, to be directly autobiographical; but it is autobiographical, according to the Proem, indirectly. For the feelings of Troiolo on the departure of Criseida from Troy are said to represent the feelings of Boccaccio on the departure of his mistress (like Criseida a widow, according to recent scholarship) from Naples. Boccaccio says that he suffered so much on this occasion that he resolved 'in persona d'alcuno passionato sì come io era e sono, cantando narrare li miei martiri. Meco adunque con sollicita cura cominciai a rivolgere l'antiche storie per trovare cui io potessi fare scudo verisimilmente del mio segreto e amoroso dolore. Né altro più atto nella mente mi venne a tale bisogno, che il valoroso giovane Troiolo . . .'.[19] This account of the genesis of Boccaccio's poem suggests a bold and novel subordination of 'antiche storie' to the private business of the love lyric.[20] It is born out by the poem itself, where we find lyric, and especially complaint, ponding on the surface of the narrative, rather as it does in the long poems of Machaut. The poem is, in fact, oriented more towards lyric than towards narrative; and Chaucer seems to have felt unhappy about this. At one point he says firmly that he is *not* writing 'de sentement':

> Forwhi to every lovere I me excuse,
> That of no sentement I this endite,
> But out of Latyn in my tonge it write.   (ii. 12–14)[21]

He preserves much of Troiolo's complaints, and even throws in a sonnet of Petrarch for good measure in one place (i. 400–20) and a song of Machaut in another (ii. 827–75). But he consistently treats his hero's sufferings as a part – albeit an important part – of the ancient story of Troilus and Cressida, which in turn forms part of the ancient story of Troy.[22] For Boccaccio, the story is a shield ('scudo') for his 'secret and amorous grief' – a grief which it both represents (as it were heraldically) and conceals. For Chaucer, as for other Ricardians, the story is the thing. *Troilus and Criseyde* is, above all, an incomparably vivid and authentic *narrative* poem.

Still more interesting, for our present purposes, is the case of the *Teseida* and the *Knight's Tale*. In the *Teseida*, as in the *Filostrato*, Boccaccio establishes from the start a lyric orientation. His letter of dedication to Fiammetta announces that his relationship with her is represented in the poem by the relationship of either Palemone or Arcita (he does not say which, but it must be Arcita) with Emilia. Chaucer might, if he wished, have preserved something of this orientation by assigning the tale to his Squire, who could well have given covert expression to his own hot love, just as Boccaccio claims to do, in the lyrical complaints of the young Theban nobles.

Instead, Chaucer assigned the tale to the Squire's father, the Knight; and we identify the Knight, not with Palamon or Arcite, but with Theseus. Theseus is a mature man, married and in the prime of life. He is also a 'conquerour' and 'lord and governour' of Athens (i. 861–2). His planet is Jupiter, ruler, according to Froissart, of a man's life between the ages of forty-six and fifty-eight, and giver of order;[23] and it is Jupiter who presides in the cosmos of the poem, as 'prince and cause of alle thyng' (i. 3036), not the Venus of Palemon or the Mars of Arcite.[24]

Chaucer's choice of narrator is an index to the way, in the *Knight's Tale* as in *Troilus*, he plays down lyrical, sentimental and quasi-autobiographical elements in his Italian source, producing a more objective, more purely 'historial' kind of poem. But the *Teseida* is a more elaborate and ambitious work than the *Filostrato*. It is a story of love; but it is also, unlike the earlier poem, a story of war – of Theseus's 'double victory' over the Amazons (Book i) and the Thebans (Book ii), and of the great tournament (Book viii). At the beginning, Boccaccio invokes Mars as well as Venus; and he claims to be the first Italian poet ever to sing of war in the vernacular. Others, he says (recalling Dante's list of the three great subjects of poetry), have sung of moral virtue and of love:

> ma tu, o libro, primo a lor cantare
> di Marte fai gli affanni sostenuti,
> nel volgar lazio più mai non veduti.
>
> (Book xii. st. 84)[25]

Boccaccio's claim to be the first Italian poet to sing of Mars is still upheld in the sixteenth century, by Trissino in his *Poetica*.[26] It is a proud claim, because war is, with love, the great subject of ancient epic narrative, of Virgil's *Aeneid* and Statius's *Thebaid*. In the *Teseida* (as the very form of its title suggests), Boccaccio aspires to match even those classic works with a lofty tale of 'fierce wars and faithful loves', just as Ariosto, Tasso and Spenser did later. To this extent the *Teseida* is, as W. P. Ker perceived, the first of the Renaissance epics;[27] and Chaucer's handling of it in the *Knight's Tale* and elsewhere therefore has a special interest for the study of Ricardian narrative.

It is clear that Chaucer was much more impressed by the *Teseida* than most modern readers have been. In *Troilus*, especially, he imitated some of its formal neo-classical features, such as the division into 'books' prefaced with invocations, or the elaborately heightened statements of time.[28] But he nowhere makes any attempt to rival Boccaccio, or Boccaccio's Latin models, in the matters of Mars. In *Troilus*, his rich narrative amplifications stop short of anything resembling a battle scene:

> And if I hadde ytaken for to write
> The armes of this ilke worthi man,
> Than wolde ich of his batailles endite;
> But for that I to writen first bigan
> Of his love, I have seyd as I kan.   (v. 1765–9)

Even in the *Knight's Tale*, where his source offered him so much that might have been appropriate to the interests of the warrior Knight, Chaucer plays down the fighting. The great battle between Athenians and Amazons, which occupies the whole of the first book of the *Teseida*, is passed over:

> And certes, if it nere to long to heere,
> I wolde have toold yow fully the manere
> How wonnen was the regne of Femenye . . . (i. 875–7)

So also is the defeat of Creon (i. 985–90), which Boccaccio again treats at length. It would seem that Chaucer did not have that sense of the 'great subject' which we find in the *Teseida* and later in so many narrative poems of the Italian, French and English Renaissance. In this region the ghost of Epic does not walk. The *Knight's Tale*, like many Ricardian poems, fails to fit comfortably into any of our categories of genre. It is certainly not epic in the neo-classical sense familiar to Dryden.[29]

Boccaccio's *Teseida* is a remarkable piece of work; but it suffers, as narrative, from a weakness which Ker attributed to all imitative or artificial epic: 'The suspicion is aroused that the author does not believe what he is telling. One feels as if trying to dream when not really asleep.'[30] This feeling, which all readers of the *Teseida* surely experience, is aroused most painfully by the battle scenes. The lack of authenticity here, the deadening literariness, make a striking contrast with the *Decameron*. One is forced to recall that Boccaccio, just as much as Guillaume de Machaut, was a 'tender man' – a civilian and a man of letters, not a warrior or a bard. Such uneasy reflections are not prompted by Chaucer's work, chiefly for the simple reason that he steers clear of fighting in his stories. It is interesting that in the two places where he does describe battles, the tournament in the *Knight's Tale* (much reduced from the *Teseida*) and the sea-fight in the Legend of Cleopatra, he modulates into an uncharacteristic manner of writing, close to that of traditional alliterative verse, as if to mark an alien matter:

> Ther shyveren shaftes upon sheeldes thikke;
> He feeleth thurgh the herte-spoon the prikke.
> Up spryngen speres twenty foot on highte;
> Out goon the swerdes as the silver brighte;
> The helmes they tohewen and toshrede;
> Out brest the blood with stierne stremes rede;
> With myghty maces the bones they tobreste.
> He thurgh the thikkeste of the throng gan threste;
> Ther stomblen steedes stronge, and doun gooth al.
>
> (i. 2605–13)[31]

Chaucer's tact in this matter is matched by the other Ricardians. Battle was one of the great traditional subjects of alliterative poetry; but neither Langland nor the *Gawain* poet shows much interest in feats of arms. Langland announces but never describes Christ's joust with Satan; and his siege of Unity is a shadowy affair. The *Gawain* poet does a vigorous siege of Jerusalem in *Purity*; but in *Sir Gawain* he passes over his hero's wars with monsters and wild animals (720–5) and concentrates on an adventure which involves, as it turns out, only one blow of an axe. As for Gower, he frequently expresses love of peace and hatred of war in his writings (e.g. *Confessio Amantis* iii. 2251 ff.); and the Confessor never lingers over fights in his stories. His cursory way with such matters can be seen in his account of the defeat of Perseus of Macedonia (ii. 1836–9), the besieging of Clytemnestra (iii. 2045–9), or the killing of the Minotaur:

> So as this maide him hadde tawht,
> Theseus with this monstre fawht,
> Smot of his hed, the which he nam . . . (v. 5359–61)

No more than Milton, then, did the Ricardian poets judge it

> chief maistry to dissect
> With long and tedious havoc fabl'd knights
> In battles feign'd. (*Paradise Lost* ix. 29–31)

Their restraint in this matter, like many other features of their work, is turned to comic effect in *Sir Thopas*, where a fight rather conspicuously fails to occur. Nevertheless, it may serve to draw our attention to the tact, calculation and artistry which went to the making of Ricardian narrative. This poetry draws much of its strength from roots which strike back into minstrel story-telling and even, in the case of alliterative verse, into remoter bardic traditions; and it is not much affected by latter-day continental developments such as the sentimental 'voir dit' or the neo-classical heroic poem of love and war. But it is not mere traditionalism which explains why the Ricardian poets were able to produce authentic narrative poetry in an age no longer favourable to it. Unlike predecessors such as the author of *Kyng Alisaunder*, they had the knack of selecting out of the mass of 'olde aproved storyes' just those episodes which they could convincingly turn to their own literary purposes.[32]

It will not be possible here to discuss in full the literary artistry displayed in Ricardian narrative. I shall therefore confine myself to three points: the formal structure of the poems, the 'pointing' (a term to be explained later) of the narrative, and the handling of theme.

II

The old way of articulating long poems in the vernaculars was to divide them up into what the Italians called 'cantos' and the English 'fitts'. In principle, the fitt simply represents the amount which a listening audience could be expected to take in without a break. But bards and minstrels did not usually chop their poems into equal sections regardless of context. They naturally favoured places where a break would be effective, either because it coincided with a break in the action or because it interrupted the action at an exciting moment. Nevertheless, these breaks do not, except rarely and as it were by accident, mark fundamental structural divisions. There is no attempt to display the deep structure of the poem (if it has one) through systematic use of breaks in the narrative; and the poem is not remembered as being articulated in any such way.[33]

English poets in the later Middle Ages still practised such division by fitt. In unskilful hands the result is arbitrary and formless.

Chaucer imitates this wickedly in *Sir Thopas*, where he breaks off in the middle of describing his hero's preparations for departure to announce the end of an uneventful and abnormally short second fitt:

> Loo, lordes myne, heere is a fit!
> If ye wol any moore of it,
> To telle it wol I fonde.   (vii. 888–90)[34]

Similar announcements mark the four fitts into which a minstrel divided *Sir Eglamour of Artois* (mid-fourteenth-century), one of the tail-rhyme romances which Chaucer imitated in *Thopas*. Only one of the three breaks in this poem is as abrupt as Chaucer's imitation; but the fitts have no consistent structural significance.[35]

By contrast, Ricardian poets show a strongly literary sense of form and structure in their handling of text-divisions. *Sir Gawain*, in the single extant manuscript, is divided into four main parts by three large illuminated capitals, each accompanied by horizontal lines running across the page.[36] These parts are commonly called 'fitts', in the absence of any guidance from text or rubric as to what the poet himself might have called them. The name can stand, provided one notes how the *Gawain* poet's fitts differ from the normal. The first is occupied, after two paragraphs of prologue, with a single long scene in which Gawain takes up the Adventure of the Green Chapel. The second, more amorphous, carries him to the eve of his critical test. The third, very tightly constructed on a principle of alternation (between bedroom and hunting-field), describes the three days of that test. The fourth, more amorphous again, concludes the Adventure. Thus two tightly unified fitts, one and three, heighten the definition of the more amorphous fitts with which they alternate, producing an exceptionally stable and well-marked four-part structure. The poet puts the audience into suspense at each break: explicitly, in the minstrel manner, at the end of fitts one and three; tacitly, as the case requires (we are left to guess the peculiar perils of 29 December), at the end of fitt two. But the breaks are fundamentally structural, not dramatic.[37]

The rubrics in the manuscripts of *Piers Plowman* divide that poem up into 'passus'. The evidence suggests that this term was regarded as the Latin equivalent of the English 'fitt';[38] but it is not surprising that the native term fails to occur. Langland, unlike such predecessors as the author of *Winner and Waster*, appears to have been little interested in the antiquities and traditions of alliterative verse. Certainly he uses his passus in the new way, to mark structural units. The prime units in his very large conception are generally too big to be contained within a single passus. These Langland encloses, as we shall see, within dreams. But passus-divisions play an important part in marking off the secondary units within these dreams. The B-text consists of a prologue and twenty passus; and there are only two places (between xiii and xiv, and between xvi and xvii) where the reader can have doubts about the structural significance of a passus-break. Otherwise the passus form clear units articulating the sense or story of the poem.

Chaucer and Gower achieve similar results in a rather different way, by dividing their poems into 'books'. The 'book' is a unit of Latin poetry, so far as the Middle Ages are concerned; and its use in vernacular poems is a definite neo-classical or learned feature.[39] Boccaccio was apparently the first to introduce it into Italian poetry when he divided the *Teseida* into the twelve books customary in epic, with the appropriate trimmings of proem and invocation. Possibly Chaucer was following his example when he divided the *House of Fame*, more modestly but still with ceremonious proems and invocations, into three 'little' books (cf. 1093).[40] Such a division seems to have been a complete novelty in English poetry around 1380. It helps to impose order upon the miscellaneous materials of Chaucer's puzzling poem: Book i, the Temple of Venus; Book ii, the journey with the Eagle; Book iii, the House of Fame and its environs. But Chaucer's masterpiece, in this respect as in others, is *Troilus and Criseyde*. *Troilus* is, indeed, the supreme example of formal articulation in Ricardian verse, surpassing even *Sir Gawain* in clarity and symmetry of structure. The five books mark out the course of Troilus's 'double sorrow'. He rises out of the sorrow of unrequited love in the first two books to the felicity of the third and central book, from which he falls into the sorrow of betrayed love in Books iv and v. Each book-division marks a definite stage in the poem's development. This is obvious in every case save one. At the end of Book ii, Chaucer breaks off abruptly in the middle of the scene at Deiphebus's house with a dramatic appeal to the audience. This may seem a somewhat arbitrary break, in the minstrel manner; but lovers in the audience are expected to see that it marks, not merely an exciting moment, but an important new stage in the inner, sentimental course of the poem:

But now to yow, ye loveres that ben here,
Was Troilus nought in a kankedort,
That lay, and myghte whisprynge of hem here,
And thoughte, 'O Lord, right now renneth my sort
Fully to deye, or han anon comfort!'
And was the firste tyme he shulde hire preye
Of love; O myghty God, what shal he seye?   (ii. 1751–7)[41]
Explicit liber secundus.

Gower's *Confessio Amantis* is also carefully articulated in the same neo-classical manner. The poem consists of a prologue and eight books. Gower does not follow Chaucer in stressing his divisions by the use of proem or invocation; but the books play an important part in the ordering of Gower's material. In each of seven books the Confessor treats one of the seven deadly sins. This is simple enough; but comparison with *Handlyng Synne,* where Robert Mannyng treats the same subject without formal divisions, shows how much Gower has gained in clarity of structure. In the one remaining book (Book vii) the Confessor turns aside from the sins to teach Amans what Aristotle taught Alexander about the speculative, rhetorical and practical sciences. Gower's editor censures this penultimate book as a 'deliberate departure from the general plan';[42] but it can be justified even from a strictly formal point of view. The effect of a single unlike member in a series of like ones is not necessarily unpleasing; and a medieval reader would not have been surprised to find a series of seven so raised to eight. The seven planetary spheres were enclosed within the sphere of the fixed stars. According to Macrobius, the monad is especially praiseworthy in conjunction with the number seven; and according to St Gregory, the raising of seven to eight signifies that 'this temporal state is brought to an end and closed by eternity'.[43] Gower's extra book may therefore be meant to point beyond the 'temporal state' represented in the other seven. 'Numerical composition' of this sort is commonplace in medieval book-poetry;[44] and it would be surprising if Ricardian poetry did not provide some examples. Scholars have made some suggestions: that the five-book structure of *Troilus* recalls the five books of Boethius's *De Consolatione Philosophiae*;[45] that the recurrence of the opening line of *Sir Gawain* in its close at line 2525 relates to the 5×5 significances of the pentangle;[46] and that the 1212 lines of *Pearl* and its twelve-line stanza relate to the dimensions of the heavenly city.[47]

Symmetry of structure and especially numerical composition belong to the bookish traditions of medieval poetry. We know that Chaucer and Gower, at least, were both bookish men. They took a keen interest in the copying of their works; and their casual use of expressions such as 'above' ('supra') instead of 'before', even where characters are speaking, shows that they thought of their work as existing on the written page.[48] At the same time – and here we detect a kind of resistance to bookishness, even in Chaucer and Gower – neither poet took advantage of the manuscript order of 'above' and 'below' to indulge in that loose, serial sort of structure in which the order of the parts depends on the goodwill and competence of scribes (and later printers). This 'book' structure was becoming popular in late medieval vernaculars. The *Libro de Buen Amor* of the fourteenth-century Spanish poet Ruiz provides an example. In this sequence of songs and stories, many of the items have no textual links with their neighbours: their position is fixed by their position in the 'libro', purely and simply.[49] The work therefore poses the question 'One work or many?', just as does Caxton's 'book of the noble histories of King Arthur', better known as Malory's *Morte Darthur*. A similar problem is presented by the so-called 'Series' of Thomas Hoccleve, where Hoccleve (himself a professional scribe) produces a literary organism which might be described as the formal equivalent of a manuscript miscellany. But the Ricardian poets themselves did not attempt 'books' of this sort. Gower, like Machaut before him, is known to have supervised the production of manuscript copies of his 'Works'; and the linking of the *Traitié pour essampler les amantz marietz* to the end of the *Confessio Amantis* in seven manuscripts by an apparently authorial rubric represents a definite step in the direction of larger composite forms.[50] One might even argue that Chaucer's Retractation, which follows the end of the *Parson's Tale* in manuscripts of the *Canterbury Tales,* represents a step in the same direction. But in general these poets produced discrete works, each with a well-marked formal structure and an unmistakable identity of its own.

Well-marked formal structure has since become almost commonplace in the English 'art tradition'; and it is difficult for modern readers to appreciate what a *new* thing Chaucer did in *Troilus and Criseyde*. But the formal structuring of Ricardian poetry has more than a historical significance. The function of the fitt in *Sir Gawain*, the passus in *Piers*, the book in *Troilus*, the *House of Fame* and the

Confessio Amantis is to enclose poetic material. Such enclosing, or encapsulation, seems to be the chief characteristic of poetic form in the age. Several devices, none in itself peculiar to the period, combine to produce this effect. Chief among them, besides the formal divisions already discussed, are the dream-vision, the framed story, and structural circularity.

Ricardian poets shared the general medieval predilection for dreams and visions; and dream-poems are common in the English poetry of this period. Chaucer's *Book of the Duchess*, *House of Fame* and *Parliament of Fowls* and the *Gawain* poet's *Pearl* are all quite conventional examples of the enclosing of poetic material in dream. Later in his career, in the *Legend of Good Women*, Chaucer experiments with the dream form, using it to provide a prologue to a set of stories – those legends of good women which, after a threatening dream, the poet wakes up to write.[51] The idea is a good one, and it is a pity that Chaucer did not complete the experiment. He might have produced a vigorous new hybrid. Another, more remarkable, experiment was made by Langland when, taking a hint perhaps from Deguileville, he coupled two dreams together (with a brief waking interval) in his *Visio*.[52] He then went on to complete a poem which, in the B-text, consists of eight dreams, two of which (a further novelty) enclose dreams-within-a-dream, making a total of ten. Langland's intention, evidently, was that each dream should enclose a dream-fiction which would have some independence structurally and thematically, while contributing at the same time to the general development of the poem. He is not successful in every case. Dreams i (marriage of Lady Mede), ii (pilgrimage to Truth), iii (search for Dowel) and viii (Harrowing of Hell) are the best constructed.[53] Dream v (Conscience's dinner-party, Hawkin) has unity of theme (patience) but not of action; Dream vi (unlike iii) is not strong enough to survive its dream-within-a-dream; and Dreams ix and x are Siamese twins. Yet the impulse is clear enough – the impulse to mark off and enclose the parts of the poem. It is this which makes the structure of *Piers* so unlike that of its nearest counterpart in French, Deguileville's *Pèlerinage de Vie Humaine*.

The same impulse contributed to the general conception of Chaucer's *Canterbury Tales* and Gower's *Confessio Amantis*, where the constituent parts are marked off not as dreams but as stories told within a 'framing' fiction. And just as Langland produces a couple of dreams-within-a-dream, so Chaucer and Gower produce stories-within-stories. Thus, the two stark and frightening little stories of prophetic dreaming in the *Nun's Priest's Tale* – the story of the corpse in the dung-cart and the story of the shipwreck – are told on the authority of 'oon of the gretteste auctour that men rede' by Chauntecleer, who is reported by the Nun's Priest, who is reported by Chaucer.[54] Similarly in *Pearl*, the poet tells the story of the Vineyard as it was told to him in his vision by the Pearl maiden on the authority of Matthew's report of Christ's words. In the *Monk's Tale*, Chaucer even presents a set of stories within a set of stories; for the Monk's series of tragedies, even if he had been allowed to complete it, would have been no more than one item in the Canterbury set. Examples of a different kind may be found in the *Book of the Duchess* and the *Parliament of Fowls*. In each of these poems the narrator, before he falls asleep and dreams, reads a story in a book: the story of Ceyx and Alcione from Ovid, and the story of Scipio from Cicero. It is sometimes suggested that Chaucer was here following a custom of the French dream poets; but this is not so.[55] On the contrary, Chaucer's inset stories seem to represent a technical innovation very characteristic of his own period. French poets such as Guillaume de Lorris introduce many secondary stories, or *exempla*, into their works; but they usually introduce them in a different way. The narrator simply digresses to tell the story, as the narrator in the *Roman de la Rose* digresses from his description of the well in the Garden of Love to tell the story of Narcissus (at l. 1437, l. 1469 in the Middle English version). This story is given no particular source (book or person) within the fiction of the poem, and therefore cannot be said to be framed or 'enclosed' as Chaucer encloses the story of Alcione. One consequence of this difference is that the bearing of Chaucer's story remains much less obvious than that of Lorris's. One sees the point of Narcissus, whose story the narrator chooses to tell, more readily than that of Alcione, whose story the narrator just happens to read. What has Alcione to do with the Man in Black? Such enigmas are more common in English poetry than in French at this (maybe at any) time. The Ricardian poem will usually have a more sharply and dramatically articulated structure, with the constituent parts marked off and enclosed; but the relationship between these parts, their bearing upon each other, may be left for the reader to discover. Such inexplicitness is especially characteristic of Chaucer. What is the relationship between the Temple of Venus and the House of Fame? Or between Scipio's dream and Chaucer's dream of Venus and Nature in the *Parliament*? Or between the *Knight's Tale* and the *Miller's Tale*? Mysteries of a similar kind confront the reader of *Piers Plowman*, where the relationship between consecutive dreams is left unspoken. The dreamer wakes up from one dream, then falls asleep and has another. The sequence, as so often in Chaucer, may seem arbitrary. Why should the dream of the pilgrimage to Truth follow the dream of the marriage of Lady Mede? We are left to guess.

The Ricardian poets' love of enclosed forms appears most strikingly in their cultivation of 'circular' structures. I call a poem 'circular' when its end is designed in one way or another to suggest to the reader that he is back at the beginning. The most obvious examples of this device are to be found in the *Gawain* manuscript. In his exposition of the Beatitudes at the beginning of *Patience*, the *Gawain* poet points out that the promise in the last (Patience) is the same as the promise in the first (Purity). In each case, Christ promises the Kingdom of Heaven:

> For in the tyxte there thyse two arn in teme layde,
> Hit arn fettled in on forme, the forme and the laste,
> And by quest of her quoyntyse enquylen on mede,
> And als, in myn upynyoun, hit arn of on kynde.   (37–40)

In the same way, the beginning and end of *Patience* itself are fastened together ('fettle' derives from an Old English word meaning 'belt') 'in on forme'; for the last line of the poem is nearly identical with the first:

> Pacience is a poynt, thagh hit displese ofte   (1)
> That pacience is a nobel poynt, thagh hit displese ofte   (531)

The effect here is simply to strengthen the frame within which the story of Jonah is set, by linking the moral reflections at the end with the moral reflections at the beginning. Thus the two passages (to use what appears to be the poet's other metaphor) pull together like oxen yoked in a team. The same linking of beginning and end 'in on forme' occurs in *Pearl* and in *Gawain*:

> Perle, plesaunte to prynces paye (*Pearl* 1)
> Ande precious perlez unto his pay   (1212)

> Sithen the sege and the assaut watz sesed at Troye   (*Gawain* 1)
> After the segge and the asaute watz sesed at Troye   (2525)[56]

In each of these cases the effect is stronger than in *Patience*. The protagonist in both poems (dreamer in *Pearl*, Gawain in *Gawain*) sets out from a familiar place (the 'erbere', Arthur's court) on an adventure (cf. *Pearl* l. 64) from which he eventually returns, a wiser man, to the familiar place – waking in the 'erbere' in *Pearl*, returning to Camelot in *Gawain*. This return to the starting-point, which does not occur in the story of Jonah, is pointed up by the verbal repetition, triumphantly in *Pearl*, soberly in *Gawain*. At the same time, in *Pearl* and perhaps in *Gawain*, the repetition has a more esoteric function. All the 101 stanzas of *Pearl* are linked together by concatenation, and by linking the last with the first in the same way the poet forges an endless chain which matches the 'endeles rounde' of the pearl (738), which in turn, as Pearl herself says, 'is lyke the reme of hevenesse clere' (735).[57] The 101 stanzas of *Gawain* are not concatenated; but the 'fettling' of end with beginning may here be meant to suggest another endless emblem – the 'endeles knot' of the pentangle on Gawain's shield, which symbolizes his perfect truth:

> For hit is a figure that haldez fyve poyntez,
> And uche lyne umbelappez and loukez in other,
> And ayquere hit is endelez.   (627–9)

The device of joining beginning and end in one form of words is not a common one in Middle English poetry.[58] It is used in two other poems which perhaps belong to our period 1370–1400, *The Awntyrs of Arthure* and the southern *Octavian*; but there are no other examples of it in the four Ricardian poets under discussion here. But the return to the starting-point, which we noted in *Pearl* and *Gawain*, is with them a common and highly characteristic kind of ending. The two dream-poems which Chaucer completed, the *Book of the Duchess* and the *Parliament of Fowls*, both end with the dreamer waking back into familiar reality, as in *Pearl*. In the *Book of the Duchess* he finds still in his hand the book from which, before falling asleep, he read the story of Alcione; while in the *Parliament* he turns, upon waking, from the *Somnium Scipionis* to 'othere bokes', in the hope of provoking a better dream:

> I hope, ywis, to rede so som day
> That I shal mete som thyng for to fare
> The bet, and thus to rede I nyl nat spare.   (697–9)

The suggestion here of repeated cycles of reading and dreaming, with no more than a hope of final repose, reminds one of the end of *Piers Plowman*. In that poem Langland rather conspicuously refrains from telling us anything about his dreamer after he wakes from the last of his many dreams: there is no return to the Malvern Hills. Yet the end of his last dream does carry us back, most readers have felt, to the beginning of the poem. It portrays the corruption of the contemporary Church, and Conscience setting out in search of the departed hero of the poem:

'Bi Cryste,' quod Conscience tho, 'I wil bicome a pilgryme,
And walken as wyde as al the worlde lasteth,
To seke Piers the Plowman, that pryde may destruye,
And that freres hadde a fyndyng that for nede flateren,
And contrepleteth me, Conscience; now Kynde me avenge,
And sende me happe and hele til I have Piers the Plowman!'
And sitthe he gradde after grace til I gan awake.   (xx. 378–84)

This circularity creates an effect very different from the 'endless round' of *Pearl*. Endlessness in *Pearl* means eternity; in *Piers* it signifies the cycle of spiritual growth and decay which will go on until the end of time, both in individuals and in institutions.[59]

The return to the starting-point appears again, with yet another significance, at the end of *Confessio Amantis*. At the beginning of Gower's poem, Amans sets out in May to walk in the woods; and it is there, in a 'swote grene pleine', that the confession takes place. In the very beautiful closing passage, Venus advises Amans to give up love and make a 'beau retret' (a graceful withdrawal, viii. 2416). She gives him a black rosary inscribed with the words *Por reposer*, and vanishes.

I stod amasid for a while,
And in my self y gan to smyle
Thenkende uppon the bedis blake,
And how they weren me betake,
For that y schulde bidde and preie.
And whanne y sigh non othre weie
Bot only that y was refusid,
Unto the lif which y hadde usid
I thoughte nevere torne ayein:
And in this wise, soth to seyn,
Homward a softe pas y wente,
Wher that with al myn hol entente

> Uppon the point that y am schryve
> I thenke bidde whil y live.   (viii. 2957–70)[60]

Gower may have had in mind the end of the dream in the *Book of the Duchess*, where the so-called 'king' (Octavian, or the Black Knight, or both) rides homewards out of the forest; for in Chaucer's poem the return home carries implicitly just those meanings which are explicit in Gower's. Octavian has lost the hart he was hunting; the Black Knight has lost his mistress; Amans is refused by his mistress. There is for each of them 'non othre weie' but to reconcile himself to realities and seek repose. Such is the significance, baldly stated, of the 'beau retret' with which both poems end.

There remains the *Canterbury Tales*. The fragmentary state of the work as we have it creates difficulties in any discussion of its form and structure. What we have comes to a kind of conclusion in the Parson's Prologue and *Tale;* but this, many people believe, represents nothing more than Chaucer's attempt to 'knit up' (cf. Pars. Prol. x. 28 and 47) a poem which, for one reason or another, he knew he would never finish. Nevertheless some critics, taking the *Parson's Tale* as the last on the outward journey, have found it satisfactory to consider the *Canterbury Tales* as a one-way pilgrimage, from London to Canterbury, or from Babylon to Jerusalem, which culminates in the Parson's exposition of:

> thilke parfit glorious pilgrymage
> That highte Jerusalem celestial.   (x. 50–1)[61]

But such a 'straight-line' structure, though it may be perceived in the extant fragments, is directly opposite in character to the 'circular' structure which, according to the present argument, we find in most poems of the period; and it would seem that Chaucer adopted it, if at all, merely as the best he could do in the circumstances. There is no reason, in other words, to doubt that he would have finished the work in accordance with the proposals made by the Host in his very explicit speech at the end of the General Prologue (i. 788 ff.). Each pilgrim is to tell two tales 'to Caunterbury-ward' and two more 'homward':

> And which of yow that bereth hym best of alle,
> That is to seyn, that telleth in this caas
> Tales of best sentence and moost solaas,

Shal have a soper at oure aller cost
Heere in this place, sittynge by this post,
Whan that we come agayn fro Caunterbury. (i. 796–801)

It is, of course, idle to speculate about what Chaucer might have made of such an ending, had he reached it; but two things may be observed about the scheme, as stated by the Host. The poem is not to end in Canterbury, still less in the Heavenly Jerusalem; it is to end where it began, in Southwark, at the Tabard, 'by this post'.[62] Further, the Host's reference to a festive supper suggests that Chaucer intended to handle this return to the starting-point in a fully comic fashion.[63] We do not find this in any of the other poems discussed here. In *Sir Gawain*, there is rejoicing at the hero's return to Camelot; but the hero himself is unconsolable, and there is, rather surprisingly, no feast, although Arthur had made a feast 'for the frekes sake' at Gawain's departure (537).

In the first section of the present chapter, I suggested that English poets are distinguished in the later Middle Ages from their French and Italian contemporaries by their predilection for sheer story-telling. However, this predilection led, in the four poets under discussion here, to results of a rather specialized kind, so far as form and structure are concerned. None of their work exhibits that species of linear form which derives, often quite naïvely in minstrel poetry, from following a hero through a long series of trials and adventures.[64] Nor do they cultivate the more complex branching or interlacing forms, where many adventures are developed together, as in the French Vulgate cycle of romances, or Malory, or Ariosto, or Spenser (especially Books iii and iv of the *Faerie Queene*). Their method is rather to isolate a single, relatively uncomplex episode, and narrate it within some strongly marked enclosed form, either as a complete work in itself *(Troilus, Sir Gawain, Patience)* or as one cell in a larger whole which in turn has a simple and well-marked shape *(Canterbury Tales, Confessio Amantis)*.

The strict formal 'enclosing' of narrative material which we find in Ricardian poetry has a parallel in the painting of the period. The combination of vigour and formality reminds one of those pages in English fourteenth-century manuscripts where little scenes bursting with action and life are contained within the shape of a big initial letter. There is an example in the frontispiece to this book. These pages and these poems balance and reconcile, Coleridge might have said, a more than usual state of energy with more than usual order.

III

So little is known of the terms in which Ricardian poets thought and spoke about their art that a special interest attaches to the few fragments of technical literary vocabulary which are to be found embedded here and there in the texts. One such term is the verb 'point', meaning 'to describe in detail'. This expression must have had some general currency since it is found both in *Sir Gawain* and in Chaucer's *Troilus*. In the single stanza which the *Gawain* poet devotes to the feasting on Christmas Day at Hautdesert, he writes:

> Bi uche grome at his degre graythely watz served
> Ther watz mete, ther watz myrthe, ther watz much ioye,
> That for to telle therof hit me tene were,
> And to poynte hit yet I pyned me paraventure.   (1006–9)

The last line has been translated: 'even if perhaps I took pains to describe it in detail'.[65] The term occurs in a similar context in *Troilus*, towards the beginning of Book iii, where Chaucer is passing over the time between Troilus's first meeting with Criseyde at the house of Deiphebus and the consummation of his love at the house of Pandarus, a period during which the lovers exchanged letters and occasionally met:

> But now, paraunter, som man wayten wolde
> That every word, or soonde, or look, or cheere
> Of Troilus that I rehercen sholde,
> In al this while unto his lady deere.
> I trowe it were a long thyng for to here;
> Or of what wight that stant in swich disjoynte,
> His wordes alle, or every look, to poynte.
>
> For sothe, I have naught herd it don er this
> In story non, ne no man here, I wene;
> And though I wolde, I koude nought, ywys;
> For ther was som epistel hem bitwene,
> That wolde, as seyth myn autour, wel contene

Neigh half this book, of which hym liste nought write.
How sholde I thanne a lyne of it endite?

But to the grete effect . . .   (iii. 491–505)

One recognizes in both these passages the familiar superlative or
'intensive' note: the feast at Hautdesert was so lavish, the letters of
Troilus and Criseyde so long, that the poets despair of reporting
them. But there is also evidence here of concern for a matter of
literary technique: what we may call the 'scale' of narrative. Scale
is not the same thing as magnitude: a large-scale map need not, in
principle, be large. Scale is the proportional relationship existing
between a representation (map, picture, narrative) and a thing represented (region, scene, event). The analogy between maps and
narratives is very imperfect; the 'scale' of a narrative is not uniform
overall, nor does the 'thing represented' in a literary narrative have
the same kind of objective, independent existence as a geographical
region. But the analogy will help us to discuss something which
might otherwise have to be called the 'level of detail' in Ricardian
narrative.

In the passage just quoted from *Troilus*, Chaucer says that he has
never heard any story in which the author 'pointed' every detail,
every word and glance of a lover. This apology comes, in fact, soon
after the most elaborately pointed episodes in medieval English
poetry – the two visits on successive May days which Pandarus
pays to Criseyde on behalf of his friend. The first of these episodes
in particular, which occupies a large part of Book ii, represents, as
Chaucer must have known, a remarkable experiment in large-scale
narrative. Although this day has few events, it is assigned as many
lines as the whole eventful *Man of Law's Tale*. Pandarus visits
Criseyde and tells her about Troilus's love; Criseyde from a window
sees Troilus ride past; she walks in her garden, goes to bed and
dreams; Pandarus reports to Troilus, who writes a letter. The
opening stanzas of this remarkable section establish its scale. We
are told that Pandarus, after a restless night, is woken by a swallow
near his window, and prepares to get up. He ascertains that the
moon is in a favourable position for travelling, and sets out for
Criseyde's house, which is nearby. When he arrives, he finds
Criseyde sitting in a paved parlour with two other ladies, listening
to the story of the siege of Thebes. In what follows Chaucer does

not, of course, point the 'wordes alle, or every look' of Pandarus and his niece; but he records much casual conversation and not a few 'looks'. Here, for example, is Pandarus preparing to tell Criseyde of her 'fair aventure':

> 'What sholde I peynte or drawen it on lengthe
> To yow, that ben my frend so feythfully?'
> And with that word he gan right inwardly
> Byholden hire and loken on hire face,
> And seyde, 'On swich a mirour goode grace!'
>
> Than thought he thus: 'If I my tale endite
> Aught harde, or make a proces any whyle,
> She shal no savour have therin but lite,
> And trowe I wolde hire in my wil bigyle;
> For tendre wittes wenen al be wyle
> Theras thei kan nought pleynly understonde;
> Forthi hire wit to serven wol I fonde' –
>
> And loked on hire in a bysi wyse,
> And she was war that he byheld hire so,
> And seyde, 'Lord! so faste ye m'avise!
> Sey ye me nevere er now – What sey ye, no?'
> 'Yis, yys,' quod he . .   (ii. 262–78)

A passage such as this represents the Ricardian art of pointing at its most elaborate. Its narrative technique is far removed from the traditions of minstrel story-telling. Among the Middle English metrical romances it could be matched only in the remarkable tail-rhyme romance *Ipomedon A,* where some scenes, such as the scene at dinner between the lady, Jason and Ipomedon (773–902), are pointed in enough detail for the reader to be reminded of Chaucer.[66] But the author of *Ipomedon A,* far from being a minstrel, was himself an exceptionally gifted writer, who might occupy a significant place in a comprehensive account of the Ricardian period. Run-of-the-mill poets come nowhere near Chaucer in delicacy of pointing technique. Not that Chaucer himself tells the whole story of Troilus on so large a scale as that which he adopts in Book ii. We have seen that he passes quite rapidly over some later stages in Troilus's wooing; and when things turn for the worse in the latter part of the story, he adopts a gloomy summary manner which contrasts with what we

by then recognize as the happy, even lyrical particularity of Books
ii and iii. The same sympathy with the hero which encouraged the
narrator to point his joys discourages him from pointing his sorrows;[67]
and he describes Troilus's death in the barest possible fashion, on a
scale which prepares for the cosmic scope of the epilogue:

> But weilawey, save only Goddes wille!
> Despitously hym slough the fierse Achille. (v. 1805–6)

In general, however, *Troilus* must count as the most elaborately
pointed of all Ricardian narratives. Its nearest rival is *Sir Gawain
and the Green Knight*. The *Gawain* poet tells a story no simpler than
Chaucer's in less than one third as many lines (*Gawain* 2530, *Troilus*
8239); and he does not attempt, within the smaller compass of his
'lay', anything as ambitious as *Troilus* Book ii. Yet he shares with
Chaucer a highly-developed technique of pointing. The three
December days which occupy his third fitt are narrated with a
brilliance of detail which rivals (though it does not equal) the two
May days in *Troilus*. This fitt opens before dawn on 29 December,
with the departure of the Christmas guests from Hautdesert. Then
we follow the Host as he eats a 'sop', hears mass, and rides out to
hunt deer. Meanwhile Gawain lies asleep, until daylight shines on to
the walls of his chamber and he wakes up to hear 'a little din at his
door' – the Lady, who has come to talk with him. The effect of this
early-morning opening is to establish both the mood and the scale
of the ensuing narrative. The mood here, as in *Troilus* when Pandarus lies half-asleep in bed, to be woken by the noisy swallow, is
peaceful and contented. Later, on the beautiful morning of 31 December, Gawain's sleep is troubled by nightmares (1750 ff.); and on
the wild, snowy morning of New Year's Day, when the hero lies
awake thinking about his coming encounter (1998 ff.), the early-
morning opening is put to chilling effect. But all such openings,
whatever their mood, establish a large scale for the ensuing narrative: they arouse desire for, and expectation of, more such detailed
narration. In the third fitt, the *Gawain* poet satisfies these expectations, both by elaborate descriptions of the hunts, where a favourite
topic is handled with unusual richness of detail, and by delicate
pointing of the morning conversations between Gawain and the
Lady. The notation of 'words and looks' in the chamber scenes is a
little stiffer and more formal than Chaucer's; but the alliterative poet
comes remarkably well out of the comparison. As each of his three

December days ends with drinking around the fire, a contemporary listener might have echoed Chaucer:

> For sothe, I have naught herd it don er this
> In story non, ne no man here, I wene.
>
> (*Troilus* iii. 498–9)

There can be no doubt that both *Troilus* and *Gawain* owe some special popularity with modern readers to their unusually elaborate pointing in scenes such as these. The May days in *Troilus* and the December days in *Gawain* will not, by their mere scale, astonish readers who have followed Leopold Bloom through the one June day which furnishes the action of *Ulysses*; but they make their appeal all the same. *Troilus* has been called the first modern novel. Yet modern readers, precisely because they are novel-readers, generally fail to appreciate the full range of the pointing techniques displayed in Ricardian narrative. They favour the large-scale narrative of *Troilus* or *Gawain* at the expense of the equally deliberate small-scale narrative to be found in the *Legend of Good Women* and in most of the stories in the *Confessio Amantis*. Smallness of scale and consequent lack of story detail ('vivid' detail) have contributed to the relative neglect of these works recently.[68]

The medieval rhetoricians, among them Geoffrey of Vinsauf, say that a writer has to choose between 'amplifying' and 'abbreviating' his material. Both amplification and abbreviation are processes of art.[69] Thus Chaucer, when he passed from *Troilus* to the *Legend*, recognized the obvious fact that his new scheme required, in general, an abbreviated, small-scale method of story-telling. Alceste herself says this at the close of her instructions to the poet:

> 'I wot wel that thou maist nat al yt ryme,
> That swiche lovers diden in hire tyme;
> It were to long to reden and to here.
> Suffiseth me thou make in this manere,
> That thou reherce of al hir lyf the grete,
> After thise olde auctours lysten for to trete.
> For whoso shal so many a storye telle,
> Sey shortly, or he shal to longe dwelle'. (F. 570–7)

This injunction to 'sey shortly' is omitted in the G-version of the Prologue, perhaps because the narrator himself makes the same point again, more vividly, in the course of telling the first of his stories, that of Cleopatra:

> The weddynge and the feste to devyse,
> To me, that have ytake swich empryse
> Of so many a story for to make,
> It were to longe, lest that I shulde slake
> Of thyng that bereth more effect and charge;
> For men may overlade a ship or barge.
> And forthy to th'effect thanne wol I skyppe,
> And al the remenaunt, I wol lete it slippe.   (616–23)

Chaucer's adoption of the *via brevitatis* in the Legends has won him little praise from modern critics: it has even been interpreted as evidence that he himself was as bored by the whole project as some of his readers have been.[70] Most people's appetite for the sheer gross matter, what Chaucer calls 'the grete', of stories such as those of Cleopatra or Thisbe is now hopelessly impaired. These stories bear for us much less 'effect and charge' than they did for a medieval audience not yet glutted with history and fiction. Yet the *via brevitatis* does at least have its own kinds of literary artifice, which we might learn to appreciate better. The light pointing of the Legends, of Gower's tales and of the shorter Canterbury tales may never appeal to modern taste as much as the heavy pointing of *Troilus* or *Sir Gawain* or, for that matter, the *Knight's Tale* or the *Miller's Tale*; but it has its own peculiar beauties, as a brief discussion of one or two instances may show.

The *Monk's Tale* is an interrupted series of 'tragedies' which itself was designed as one of the larger series of more than a hundred Canterbury tales. At the end of the fifty-six-line tragedy of Ugolino of Pisa, Chaucer refers the reader to Dante for more details:

> Of this tragedie it oghte ynough suffise;
> Whoso wol here it in a lenger wise,
> Redeth the grete poete of Ytaille
> That highte Dant, for he kan al devyse
> Fro point to point, nat o word wol he faille.
>
> (vii. 2458–62)

The 'lenger wise' of some of the other Canterbury tales is not possible here. The Monk cannot tell each of his stories 'fro point to point'. Yet there is a kind of pointing in these minuscule stories.

The tiny cells are not without a life of their own. At the end of the tragedy of Nero, for example, the Emperor, pursued at night by the angry people of Rome, takes refuge in a garden.

> And in this gardyn foond he cherles tweye
> That seten by a fyr ful greet and reed.
> And to thise cherles two he gan to preye
> To sleen hym, and to girden of his heed. (vii. 2543–6)

The two unidentified churls sitting at night (why?) in a garden by a great fire, whose redness implies the surrounding black, create a vivid and slightly sinister image of stillness, contrasting with the desperate and pitiable activity of Nero. It is the description of the fire, consisting of nothing more than a couple of simple, primary epithets, which brings the scene alive. By a single touch of pointing in a generally unpointed tale, Chaucer creates a moment of narrative as authentic and memorable, in its way, as any in Ricardian poetry. It is unlike anything in *Gawain* or *Troilus*, for it has a kind of abstractness which can only be achieved in small-scale narrative.

The *Canterbury Tales* exhibits many degrees of pointing, ranging from the tiny scale of some of the Monk's tragedies (a single stanza only, in four cases) up to the rich elaboration of the *Knight's Tale*. Among the *fabliau* tales, for example, the *Shipman's Tale* exhibits a different degree of pointing from the *Miller's Tale*. The Miller introduces three of his four principle characters (Nicholas, Alison, Absolon) in set descriptions whose vividness and particularity has made them famous. The Shipman, on the other hand, introduces his principal briefly, in pointed but generalized phrases. The merchant is 'riche . . . for which men helde him wys'; the wife, 'of excellent beautee, and compaignable and revelous was she'; the monk Daun John (the only character in the tale with a name), 'a fair man and a boold'. The *Miller's Tale* continues throughout in a 'lenger wise' of narrative than the *Shipman's Tale;* and this is no doubt one reason why the latter tale has struck many readers as lacking, comparatively, in colour and life. Yet it is, in truth, a masterpiece of restrained and economical pointing. The monk's state of sexual desire, for instance, is established by a single word and look:

> 'But deere nece, why be ye so pale?
> I trowe, certes, that oure goode man
> Hath yow laboured sith the nyght bigan,

That yow were nede to resten hastily.'
And with that word he lough ful murily,
And of his owene thought he wax al reed.

(vii. 106–11)

'Laboured' is perfect, and so is the laugh which the word provokes, and the blush which overtakes the laugh. The same precision and economy of touch appear almost everywhere else in the tale. We are told just enough, for example, about the merchant's business affairs, which take him, as the story requires, first to Bruges and then back home to St Denis and on to Paris, to satisfy any demands which the scale of this particular narrative might encourage. An unexpectedly large purchase of 'ware' in Bruges, we are told, forces the merchant to raise a short-term loan, which he then has to repay in Paris at another branch of the same Lombard bank. On his way to Paris, he calls in at St Denis to pick up what ready cash he has about the house, so that he can minimize the new long-term debt which he will incur in Paris when he repays the Lombards. This sequence of events is touched in lightly and expertly in a number of passages (vii. 302–6, 325–34, 343–8, 365–8). It is characteristic of this tale that we are told exactly how much money was involved in the merchant's deal, but not what merchandise.

Gower generally works on a smaller scale than this, even in his longest stories: the story of Apollonius, which occupies much (1,740 lines) of his last book, derives its length from a long and complex chain of incident, not from detailed pointing. His mastery of small-scale narrative may be illustrated from the tale of Albinus and Rosemund (Book i, ll. 2459–646). The festival which Albinus makes in honour of his wife is introduced by a brief account of preparations:

> The grete stiedes were assaied
> For joustinge and for tornement,
> And many a perled garnement
> Embroudred was ayein the dai.   (i. 2508–11)

The abstract, generalizing manner, marked by Gower's special use of definite and indefinite articles, creates a context in which the epithet 'perled' produces an exquisite effect. The account of the jousting and feasting which follows is equally general and unspecific ('On jousteth wel, an other bet', 'And thus benethe and ek above / Al was

76

of armes and of love'), until we come to the fatal cup, which Albinus
has made out of the skull of his wife's conquered father:

> Which mad was of Gurmoundes hed,
> As ye have herd, whan he was ded,
> And was with gold and riche stones
> Beset and bounde for the nones,
> And stod upon a fot on heihte
> Of burned gold, and with gret sleihte
> Of werkmanschipe it was begrave
> Of such werk as it scholde have,
> And was policed ek so clene
> That no signe of the skulle is sene,
> But as it were a gripes ey.   (2535-45)

Gower's vagueness about the workmanship of the cup ('Of such
werk as it scholde have') prepares for the startling precision of the
last detail: a spot of exposed bone the size of a griffin's egg.[71] A
modern reader will be reminded of the sudden close-up which may,
in films, create a similar horrific effect.

These examples from Chaucer and Gower suggest some of the
artistic possibilities of light pointing as practised by Ricardian
poets. But it would be wrong to try to give the impression that detail
is always functional in their work. Indeed the modern reader may
be more struck by these poets' readiness, even in small-scale narrative, to enlarge on some time-honoured topic of description simply
for the love of it: topics such as the armed man and the beautiful
woman, the spring landscape, the feast, the voyage and the hunt.
These descriptions are usually very literary in character, whether or
not the influence of the rhetoricians is apparent in them; and their
appearance in abbreviated narrative often creates a peculiarly sophis-
ticated effect. Examples of this mannerism may be found in alliterative verse (the sea-voyage in *Patience*, or the orchard in *Susannah*);
but it is more common in Chaucer and Gower. Thus Gower finds
space, in the course of a forty-four line version of Actaeon's death,
for a tiny decorative description of the forest landscape:

> He syh upon the grene gras
> The faire freisshe floures springe,
> He herde among the leves singe
> The throstle with the nyhtingale.   (i. 352-5)

77

Chaucer amuses himself with this herb-and-bird formula in *Sir Thopas* (vii. 760–71); but he himself, as every reader knows, went to considerable lengths in rhetorical description. A remarkable example occurs in the first of the stories in the *Legend of Good Women*, the Legend of Cleopatra. Chaucer passes over Cleopatra's wedding-feast with the observation (quoted above, p. 74) that 'men may over-lade a ship or barge'; yet a moment later he devotes fully fifteen lines to a detailed description of the sea-fight in which Antony was defeated:

> Up goth the trompe, and for to shoute and shete,
> And peynen hem to sette on with the sunne.
> With grysely soun out goth the grete gonne,
> And heterly they hurtelen al atones,
> And from the top doun come the grete stones.
> In goth the grapenel . . . etc.   (635–40)

The passage is a *tour de force*, in something like Gower's generalizing manner, on a traditional topic;[72] yet it undoubtedly 'overloads' this particular tale of Cleopatra's martyrdom in love's cause. There is something here of that mannerism which Curtius discusses in his book *European Literature and the Latin Middle Ages*: 'In manneristic epochs, the *ornatus* is piled on indiscriminately and meaninglessly. In rhetoric itself . . . lies concealed one of the seeds of Mannerism. It produces a luxuriant growth in Late Antiquity and the Middle Ages.'[73]

IV

The literary sophistication which appears in the structuring and pointing of Ricardian narrative poetry appears also in the poets' handling of the meaning and signification of their stories. We shall be concerned here, not with the significations themselves, but with what medieval theorists of language called the *modus significandi*, or 'manner of signifying'. Ricardian poets did not tell stories for their own sake, they would have said, nor merely for the sake of the 'mirth and solace' in them. They proposed, in nearly every case, a signification for the story. What was their manner of signifying?

The Middle Ages has a well-deserved reputation for allegory; and readers of English poetry, when they venture back into the fourteenth century, may be haunted by the suspicion that they are there debarred from some deep and important 'level' of meaning accessible only to trained medievalists. Now it goes without saying that many particular significances, including some allegories, will escape the common reader in Ricardian, as in other, poetry. But the prevailing *modus significandi* in this period is *not* the allegorical mode. Few of the fictions of Ricardian poetry, that is, have their main meaning in some sphere of signification other *(allos)* than that which the story itself literally occupies. The basic mode of meaning is literal, not tropical; and the intentions of the poet are, to that extent, clear for the modern reader to see. Not that readers of Ricardian narrative can afford to forget all about allegory. Allegory is present in various forms. Sometimes it is explicit, as in *Pearl*, where the pearl which the maiden wears on her breast, identified with the pearl of price bought by the merchant in the parable, is said by the maiden herself to be:

> lyke the reme of hevenesse clere:
> So sayde the Fader of folde and flode;
> For hit is wemles, clene, and clere,
> And endeles rounde.   (735–38)

Sometimes the allegory is inexplicit, as in the opening section of the same poem, where the loss of the pearl in the grassy place clearly represents something other than itself, most probably the loss of a beloved child; or in the *Book of the Duchess*, where Octavian's hunt seems to have a significance, allegorically, for the grieving Black Knight.[74] Such cases as the last are of their nature controversial; but they offer possibilities of allegorical meaning to which no reader should close his mind, not even in the name of common sense.

On the other hand, Ricardian poets tend to favour literal over metaphorical modes of meaning even in works which we would call allegories. Chaucer's *Tale of Melibee*, for instance, tells of a young man called Melibeus ('a man that drinketh honey', i.e. enjoys worldly prosperity, vii. 1410–12) who suffers an assault on his wife Prudence and his daughter Sophie (wisdom) by three 'old foes' who climb into his house and wound his daughter in five places. The names of the persons, together with the schematic nature of the action, prepare us for the interpretation which Prudence herself announces to Melibee:

Thou hast doon synne agayn oure Lord Crist; for certes, the three enemys of mankynde, that is to seyn, the flessh, the

79

feend, and the world, thou hast suffred hem entre in to thyn
herte wilfully by the wyndowes of thy body, and hast nat
defended thyself suffisantly agayns hire assautes and hire
temptaciouns, so that they han wounded thy soule in fyve
places; this is to seyn, the deedly synnes that been entred
into thyn herte by thy fyve wittes.

But at this point, Prudence's exposition takes an unexpected turn:
'And in the same manere oure Lord Crist hath woold and suffred
that thy three enemys been entred into thyn house by the wyndowes, and han ywounded thy doghter in the forseyde manere.'
(vii. 1420–6).[75] Thus the assault on Melibee's household is represented as a real event which, by a kind of poetic justice, follows the
(metaphoric) pattern of Melibee's sin. Only because the assault is
'real' does the question of vengeance arise – the question which
occupies the greater part of the tale. The lengthy discussions of this
subject show that the case is being taken literally: it does not make
sense to revenge oneself upon, or forgive, 'the flesh, the fiend, and
the world'. Prudence, accordingly, figures chiefly as a prudent wife,
rather as Justinus and Placebo in the *Merchant's Tale* represent,
respectively, a plainspeaker and a flatterer. So Harry Bailey's robustly
literal reaction to Chaucer's story is not as ridiculous as some
critics (more medieval than the Middle Ages) would have us
believe:

> Whan ended was my tale of Melibee,
> And of Prudence and hire benignytee,
> Oure Hooste seyde, 'As I am feithful man,
> And by that precious corpus Madrian,
> I hadde levere than a barel ale
> That Goodelief, my wyf, hadde herd this tale!
> For she nys no thyng of swich pacience
> As was this Melibeus wyf Prudence.'   (vii. 1889–96)[76]

A similar predilection for literal modes of meaning can be detected
even in the great allegory of *Piers Plowman*. For the first of his
dreams (up to the end of Passus iv in the B-text), Langland devised
the story of the marriage of Lady Mede. The chief mode of meaning
here is unquestionably allegorical: the marriage of Mede to False
or to Conscience would represent, among other things, the reward-
ing either of the crook or of the just man with the prosperity of this
world. But neither marriage in fact takes place. By the end of the

dream, indeed, the whole matter of the marriage, so dramatically introduced in Passus ii, has been almost forgotten. Instead, in Passus iv, interest is redirected to the complaint which Peace brings against Wrong before the King and his counsellors, Conscience and Reason. This confusing shift in the action of the dream proves, on inspection, to represent a change from the allegorical to the literal mode. The 'allegorical' names of Peace and Wrong do not conceal the fact that their case before the King is simply an example, a real-life, literal example, of a situation where the issues raised by Mede – issues of reward, bribery and due punishment – are at stake. When the King refuses bribes from the wealthy and powerful defendant and condemns him to irons, we see literally what would have been signified allegorically if Mede had been given to Conscience in marriage: due reward for the just, due punishment for the unjust. But Langland has by this time abandoned his allegory and degraded Mede.

The same 'literalism' appears again under different circumstances in the second dream (Passus v–vii). The story of this dream concerns Reason's sermon to the people, their confession and pilgrimage to Truth, and the pardon which Truth grants them. This story is truly allegorical insofar as it represents Langland's vision of a possible, partial reformation or conversion of society; but it is less radically allegorical than the story of Mede's marriage, because it includes events which would actually have a place in such a conversion. The great public sermon followed by mass repentance and confession formed, indeed, the classic pattern of social reformation in the Middle Ages; and Langland no doubt hoped that the pestilences and other natural disasters of his own day (see v. 13–20) would set off just such a process in England. But this same partially literal understanding of his allegory creates difficulties for the poet once he reaches the third stage of his chosen action, the pilgrimage to Truth announced by Reason (v. 58) and undertaken by the penitent people as a penance for their sins. For Langland could not endorse pilgrimages in literal fact, as he endorsed preaching and confession. Considered as an allegory, the pilgrimage is unexceptionable, representing as it does the life of virtue lived according to the ten commandments and leading to God. But Langland sees it also as an example – an example, literally taken, of what he regarded as the profitless visiting of saints' shrines. So, through the instrumentality of Piers, he diverts the people from their pilgrimage to work on the half-acre. The episode of the half-acre is a true, literal example of that good life which the now-discarded pilgrimage would have signified allegorically. It takes the place of the pilgrimage, and achieves the latter's end: a pardon. Once more, Langland has shifted into a basically literal mode of signification.[77]

If it be granted that the prevailing *modus significandi* in Ricardian narrative is not allegorical but literal, it remains to define this literal mode more exactly. Do these poets favour any particular literal mode? An affirmative answer is ready to hand, suggested by the three cases just considered and confirmed in the work of all four poets. Their work exhibits just that 'marked emphasis on the exemplary aspects of the story' which, according to Mehl, is characteristic of the Middle English romances.[78] Their favoured mode is exemplification. A story, for them, is pre-eminently an example which illustrates some truth or concept concerning human life and conduct. Their stories exhibit more than the general representative significance which, admittedly, attaches to any literary fiction whatsoever. They are designed to exemplify some specific idea. Often this idea is stated quite explicitly, as in story-collections such as the *Monk's Tale*, the *Legend of Good Women* or *Confessio Amantis*, or in individual stories such as *Patience* or *Purity*; but even where it is not so stated, it generally proves to be susceptible of precise, even formal, definition.

The Ricardian poets lived in an age of analysis, in the aftermath of scholasticism. Habits of distinguishing, defining, classifying and schematizing had spread out from the universities to establish themselves, often in much coarsened forms, in the common mind. Scholastic moral philosophy, in particular, encouraged the development of those confessional manuals, very influential from the second quarter of the thirteenth century onwards, which brought schematic analysis to the disorderly territory of human character and motive in which the story-teller worked.[79] In the age which produced the *Parson's Tale* it is not surprising to find poets exercising strict control over the moral bearings of a story. These poets' preference, noted earlier, for relatively simple stories, as against complex or serial ones, finds an explanation here. They were interested not so much in the history of an individual, a court or a nation, as in moral ideas. Hence we might expect to find a preponderance of single-episode stories, given the relative ease with which the moral bearing of such tales can be controlled and limited. Like

the authors of clerical *exempla*, these poets are governed by a principle of selection which requires them to pick out individual episodes
from existing cycles and series, as the *Gawain* poet picked out the
Adventure of the Green Chapel from the cycle of tales about
the Round Table. The life of Gawain is not his subject, still less
the history of the Round Table.

The exemplary mode is not very attractive to modern readers. We
have been taught by so many good critics to respond sympathetically
and intelligently to allegorical stories that the allegorical mode has
once more become acceptable; but stories which represent themselves as 'examples', whether in medieval or in Renaissance literature, are something of an embarrassment. There are good reasons
for this. In a fiction which merely exemplifies an ethical concept
('patience', 'gluttony') or an accepted truth ('Women are fickle',
Radix malorum est cupiditas), literature condemns itself to an ancil-
lary role as the servant of the moral or political or religious beliefs
of its age. The process of metaphorical transfer, or *translatio*, necessary to allegory ensures, we may feel, some degree of imaginative
independence in that mode; but in the literal mode of 'exemplification', the story may do no more than illustrate slavishly *idées reçues*.
Such is indeed the case with most of the illustrative stories, or
exempla, to be found in medieval sermons and books of religious
instruction.[80] Ideally, these stories just illustrate the writer's or the
preacher's point. Any obliquity in their bearing on that point, any
unexpected implication, any irony or wit, will strike us as merely
unintentional and unfortunate. The writer always tries to select
obvious, unequivocal examples to make his point; but he does not
always succeed. Such didactic writers, even when they command
an elegant or forceful style, are of very limited interest.

Considerations such as these explain why relatively little attention
has been paid to the relation between Ricardian stories and the ideas
which, more or less explicitly, they exemplify. It is often assumed
that this relationship is at best obvious, at worst clumsy and forced,
as if these poets were, in this respect, little better than their clerical
predecessors. In *Confessio Amantis*, for example, we recognize the
individual merits of many of the stories which Genius tells Amans in
the course of his confession; but how many readers are prepared to
recognize felicity, or wit, or profundity, in the application of these
stories? But felicity, wit and even profundity are all to be found there;
for Gower, like some of his contemporaries, brings imagination

and finesse to the old didactic mode. His examples cannot be taken for granted as flat illustrations. The relationship between the story and its prescribed signification within the schema of the seven deadly sins is something for the reader to think about. It challenges him to an intellectual response, almost like the relationship between tenor and vehicle in a metaphysical conceit.

The section on 'lachesse' in *Confessio Amantis* provides typical examples of the way Gower finesses with his illustrative stories. At the beginning of this section, Amans confesses to 'lachesse' (tarrying or procrastination) in love: because he is timid and bashful, he has continually put off speaking to his lady of his love. In response, Genius tells two 'olde ensamples' (cf. iv. 75) of the evils of delay in matters of love, both based on Ovid's *Heroides*: how Aeneas tarried away from the faithful Dido, and how Ulysses distressed the faithful Penelope by tarrying at the siege of Troy. He adds two brief illustrations of the evils of delay in other matters: how the 'great clerk' Grosseteste lost the labour of seven years by a delay of half a minute, and how the Foolish Virgins missed the wedding. By simply bringing together four such heterogeneous tales – two Ovidian stories of antiquity, a scriptural parable and a 'modern instance' (Grosseteste was a thirteenth-century Bishop of Lincoln) – Gower creates a primary effect of wit and ingeniousness. What, the riddle might run, do Aeneas, Ulysses, Bishop Grosseteste and the Foolish Virgins have in common? But there is also humour, in the relation of the two Ovidian examples to the lover's case. Aeneas and Ulysses each enjoyed the devotion of his lady, and any 'lachesse' in such circumstances is unintelligible to Amans. He would not delay for a moment, he ruefully tells Genius, if only his mistress would take the slightest notice of him:

> I wolde I were unjoynted
> Of every lime that I have,
> If I ne scholde kepe and save
> Min houre bothe and ek my stede,
> If my ladi it hadde bede.
> Bot sche is otherwise avised.   (iv. 274–79)

Beyond this humour, again, lie possibilities of irony. Both Aeneas and Ulysses were 'delayed' by high duties, the founding of Rome and the taking of Troy. Perhaps, therefore, a thinking reader should reject the Confessor's equation between 'lachesse in loves cas' and the sloth of the Foolish Virgins. Perhaps – though Venus's Confessor does not say so – 'lachesse in loves cas' is not a vice at all. In such ways as these, Gower's collection of *exempla* demands from the reader an alertness to context and implication, a readiness to see wit and point in the application of a story. The stories themselves are often quite unremarkable; and it is not surprising that some people who read Gower for the individual brilliancy of his stories, without attending to their exemplary point, should find him, as Coleridge did, 'insufferably dull'. A section such as that on 'lachesse' offers none of those special beauties of story-telling so often cited by Gower's admirers.

The same literal mode of exemplification prevails in the poems of the *Gawain* manuscript. Two of these pieces, *Patience* and *Purity*, are particularly close (as their modern editorial titles suggest) to clerical traditions of the moral *exemplum*. *Patience*, the more simply constructed and possibly the earlier of the two,[81] tells the story of Jonah as an example of impatience to show what patience is. The topic is stated explicitly in prologue and epilogue, and the poet addresses the reader in the direct manner of a preacher:

> Pacience is a poynt, thagh hit displese ofte.
> When hevy herttes ben hurt wyth hethyng other elles,
> Suffraunce may aswagen hem and the swelme lethe.   (1–3)

Patience is simple, grave and straightforward, by comparison with *Confessio Amantis*. Its distinction, considered as an *exemplum*, lies in the selection of a story which draws attention away from the more obvious and exterior conceptions of patience (such as might have been suggested by the story of Job) towards a thoroughly inward conception of 'steering the heart' (l. 27).[82] *Purity* is an altogether more ambitious exercise in the same manner. Because of its more extensive treatment of biblical stories, *Purity* has sometimes been compared with Anglo-Saxon 'biblical epics' such as *Genesis*. But there is a basic difference. The Middle English poet, as was customary in his age, selects his materials and orders them not on historical but on thematic principles. The main theme, stated clearly at the beginning and end, as in *Patience*, is 'clannesse'; and the poet picks out and combines three historically separate biblical episodes to illustrate it – or rather, as in *Patience*, its opposite – in three ways ('upon thrynne wyses', l. 1805). The first two episodes, the Flood and the Destruction of Sodom and Gomorrah, simply illustrate

God's anger against various kinds of sexual uncleanness; but the third and longest episode, the Fall of Belshazzar, challenges the reader to a broader understanding of the poem's theme. Its inclusion, as Menner explains in his edition of the poem, 'is due to the wide application of the word *clannesse*, which comprises not only chastity, but purity in the sense of freedom from any defilement. It is thus that Belshazzar, who defiles the sacred vessels of God at his impious feast, becomes a sinner against *clannesse* or purity'.[83] Elsewhere Menner points out a further subtlety in the conception of the poem, observing that a secondary theme of 'trawthe' is entwined with the main theme: besides the three examples of uncleanness, there are four examples of untruth, Lucifer, Adam, Lot's wife and the people of Jerusalem.[84] Such observations support Menner's conclusion that *Purity* is 'worked out with elaborate care'. The poet's failure – surprising in this period – to give cellular form to his series of examples by 'enclosing' them leaves the exterior form of his poem somewhat rambling and unsatisfactory; but the inner relations of its constituent parts show a mastery of the exemplary mode.

In *Sir Gawain and the Green Knight* the poet does not introduce his story as illustration of a virtue. His historical prologue presents the story, rather, as a specimen of the marvels of Britain in general and of Arthurian Britain in particular: 'an outtrage awenture of Arthurez wonderez'. Yet his selection and handling of this episode from the Arthurian cycle, like his selections from the Old Testament cycle in *Purity*, prove to be governed, at least in part, by considerations of moral theme. His version of the Adventure of the Green Chapel is so full of spontaneous and unpredictable energy that we may fail to notice at first how its significances as a moral example offer themselves for precise definition. The pentangle on Gawain's shield is, the poet says, a 'token of *trawthe*' (cf. 626); and this 'truth' proves to be the common and chief issue in the tests to which the hero is submitted.[85] If the poem were to be called any such thing, it should be called *Truth*. But the title would be an unhappy one, partly because of the presence of other moral issues entwined, here more intricately than in *Purity*, with the chief issue. Gawain's fidelity to his word, pledged to the Green Knight and later (in the Exchange of Winnings) to the Host, is variously endangered, in the dense fictional world of the poem, by such factors as his courteous weakness for women and especially his desire not to die. Out of all this the poet builds a hierarchy of moral issues, based on scholastic principles of subordination, with 'trawthe' at the top. Gawain himself spells out something of the exemplary significance of his adventure in a speech which may, for its baldness of explanation, remind us of the speeches of cock and fox at the end of the *Nun's Priest's Tale*:

> For care of thy knokke cowardyse me taght
> To acorde me with covetyse, my kynde to forsake,
> That is larges and lewte that longez to knyghtez.
> Now am I fawty and falce, and ferde haf ben ever
> Of trecherye and untrawthe: bothe bityde sorwe
> and care!   (2379–84)

But this speech forms only one element in an ending which is itself bold and original. Normally in the *exemplum* tradition the relation between story and virtue is unequivocal; an example is either good or bad, how to do it or how not to do it. The Confessor in Gower works on this simple binary system, and so does the *Gawain* poet himself in *Patience* and *Purity*; Jonah, Belshazzar and the rest are notable examples of *im*patience and *im*purity. But in *Sir Gawain*, this easy either-or response is inhibited. To Bertilak, to the court and to the reader, Gawain represents his own conduct in the adventure as an example of 'trecherye and untrawthe'. Yet Bertilak and, by implication, the court represent that same conduct as an example of 'grete trauthe' (2470). Which are we to believe? The answer, whatever it may be, is not simple. Neither of the parties is merely wrong. Gawain has failed in truth, more seriously than a modern reader may realize; yet he has done well, too – better, certainly, that we could hope to do. So we may come to see the story as an example, not in the last analysis of 'truth', but of the capacities and limitations of man. At any rate, the poet, working within the mode of exemplification, achieves results far beyond the reach of the clerical prototype.

By contrast, Langland appears for once rather conventional. We have already looked at two straightforward examples in the *Visio*: the case of Peace and Wrong, and the episode of the half-acre. In the *Vita*, Langland's sporadic narrative of the life of Christ provides a further illustration. Here Langland is chiefly concerned neither with allegorical interpretations of the life of Christ, nor with that life as a historical event with its own continuity and consequences.

Instead, he selects from the canonical and apocryphal gospels those episodes in the story which exemplify certain moral ideas. From Passus xvi (where the *Vita Christi* begins, at l. 90, with the Annunciation) to Passus xviii (which culminates in the Resurrection), Langland's chief concern is with the idea of charity, already introduced by Anima in Passus xv. In these passus, Christ figures chiefly as an example of charity, side by side with Abraham, the example of faith, and Moses, the example of hope. In the account of his ministry, his healing miracles are stressed (xvi. 103–18) rather than his teaching. He is identified with the Good Samaritan (xvii. 48–79).[86] The chief event in Passus xviii is the Harrowing of Hell, a supreme example of active mercy and love. There follows at the beginning of Passus xix a long and difficult speech (26–193) in which Conscience reviews the life of Christ once more for the benefit of Will. Towards the end of this speech (104 ff.), Conscience attempts to show that Christ exemplified successively in the course of his life the 'three lives' of the *Vita*. At the marriage in Cana, when he turned water into wine and so taught symbolically the law of love, he began to 'dowel' (112); when he worked his healing miracles, he 'caughte a gretter name, the whiche was dobet' (124–25); and when after his Resurrection he granted the power of the keys to Peter, 'dobest he taughte' (177). All this has the air of a clever improvization. Conscience's speech offers the equivalent, in the exemplary mode, of a conceit.

Chaucer is distinguished from Langland and from the *Gawain* poet by his strong tendency to fictionalize the process of exemplification itself. Chaucer brings into question the teller of the *exemplum* and his motives, as well as those of his audience, rather as Gower does in *Confessio Amantis* but to much more subversive effect. When the Host appoints himself 'juge and reportour' of the pilgrims at the beginning of the *Canterbury Tales*, he announces that he will award the prize to 'tales of best sentence and moost solaas' (i. 798). A 'tale of sentence', for him, is a story which illustrates some general truth which has an immediate bearing on his own daily life. Thus he approves of Chaucer's *Tale of Melibee* because the patience of Prudence would serve as a good example to his own unruly wife Goodelief (vii. 1891–1922). At the end of the *Merchant's Tale*, he is again thinking of Goodelief (iv. 2419–40). Taking the tale as an example of the 'sleightes and subtilitees' of women, he reflects that his own wife, for all her many faults, is at least faithful. From the

Shipman's Tale he derives a less personal, but still very down-to-earth, conclusion: 'Draweth no monkes moore unto youre in' (vii. 442). This is similar to the conclusion which the Cook derives from the *Reeve's Tale*, which he sees as a modern example of an ancient truth:

> Wel seyde Salomon in his langage,
> 'Ne bryng nat every man into thyn hous';
> For herberwyng by nyghte is perilous.
> Wel oghte a man avysed for to be
> Whom that he broghte into his pryvetee. (i. 4330–4)

Such reactions offer no positive guidance to the reader in his own responses to the tales. They suggest only the sceptical thought that his own circumstances and preoccupations will determine also what he sees in a tale. Harry Bailey, a professionally hospitable man, sees in the Shipman's story an example of what may happen if one is hospitable to monks. Such is the opinion of the appointed 'juge and reportour' of the tales; and it is hard to be sure that our own opinions will be any better.

If listeners use stories for their own private purposes, so, of course, do the story-tellers. The most outrageous case of this on the Canterbury pilgrimage is the Pardoner. He describes how he uses a formal *exemplum* against avarice as a means, precisely, of making money. Another professional preacher, the Friar, also attacks an evil which is precisely his own, in his *exemplum* of the summoner and the devil. He himself, as the General Prologue reports, is adept at squeezing money out of poor widows (i. 253–5); yet that is just what, in his story, the summoner goes to Hell for (iii. 1573–8). Again, when the Friar has finished his story, the Summoner on the pilgrimage angrily responds with the story of a friar who, after preaching on the evils of wrath to an angry man and telling three examples out of Seneca (iii. 2017 ff.), himself falls into a great rage.

The Pardoner grossly misuses his *exemplum* for venal ends; but other tellers have less culpable motives. Chaucer himself, after submitting rather ingloriously to the Host's rough interruption of *Sir Thopas*, shows in *Melibee* how glorious it is to submit; the Merchant, who has recently made an unfortunate marriage, tells a tale of the miseries of matrimony; the Franklin, reminded by the Squire of his own son's lack of virtue and gentillesse, tells a tale which illustrates those qualities; the Wife of Bath shows what it is for women to have sovereignty in marriage; the Clerk replies with his tale of Griselda. These pilgrims are not to be condemned; but our knowledge of their motives is sufficient to deflect, to a greater or less degree, the exemplary bearing of their tales. They do not speak directly to us, as does the narrator in *Patience* and (often) *Piers Plowman*, but obliquely to a fictional audience. The exemplary mode is present everywhere in the *Canterbury Tales*, but everywhere subverted. The subversive spirit finds its fullest expression in the tale of a pilgrim about whose character and motives we are told very little – the Nun's Priest. His story ends very much in the clerical manner. A moral issues, as if within a scroll, from the mouths of Chauntecleer – 'For he that wynketh, whan he sholde see, / Al wilfully, God lat him nevere thee' – and of Russell – 'God yeve hym meschaunce, / That is so undiscreet of governaunce / That jangleth whan he sholde holde his pees.' Then the Priest addresses a few final words to the 'goode men' of his audience:

> But ye that holden this tale a folye,
> As of a fox, or of a cok and hen,
> Taketh the moralite, goode men.   (vii. 3438–40)[87]

But the effect is unlike the end of, say, *Patience*, for we are left asking, What *is* the morality? 'Keep your eyes open and your mouth shut' might do for the *Manciple's Tale*, but not for the Nun's Priest's. This problem of what the Nun's Priest means strikes many readers as a characteristically Chaucerian problem, and surely this impression is correct. The elusive way of working within the exemplary mode, not characteristic of his contemporaries, though there are traces of it in Gower, may be recognized in almost all Chaucer's work from the *Book of the Duchess* onwards. The *Legend of Good Women*, considered in relation to *Troilus and Criseyde*, will provide one more illustration.

Towards the end of *Troilus*, Chaucer addresses the 'bright' and 'gentil' women in his audience. His story of Criseyde's infidelity, he says, is not meant to be offensive. He would much rather write about faithful women such as Alceste or Penelope. Indeed, the present story is directed rather against male than against female infidelity:

> N'y sey nat this al oonly for thise men,
> But moost for wommen that bitraised be

Thorugh false folk; God yeve hem sorwe, amen!
That with hire grete wit and subtilte
Bytraise yow! And this commeveth me
To speke, and in effect yow alle I preye,
Beth war of men, and herkneth what I seye. (v. 1779–85)

This extraordinary stanza anticipates the jaunty conclusion to the
Legend of Phyllis: 'Be war, ye wemen, of youre subtyl fo . . . And
trusteth, as in love, no man but me' (*LGW* 2559–61). More than
that, it contains the germ of the whole *Legend of Good Women*. In
the Prologue to that work, we are invited to believe that polite
readers, rejecting Chaucer's apology at the end of *Troilus*, have
understood that work as an *exemplum* of female infidelity. It is for
these readers that the God of Love speaks when he accuses the
poet:

Hast thow nat mad in Englysh ek the bok
How that Crisseyde Troylus forsok,
In shewynge how that wemen han don mis?
But natheles, answere me now to this,
Why noldest thow as wel han seyd goodnesse
Of wemen, as thow hast seyd wikednesse?
Was there no good matere in thy mynde,
Ne in alle thy bokes ne coudest thow nat fynde
Som story of wemen that were goode and trewe?

(G 264–72)

The poet, in reply, defends *Troilus*:

what so myn auctour mente,
Algate, God wot, it was myn entente
To forthere trouthe in love and it cheryce,
And to be war fro falsnesse and fro vice
By swich ensumple.   (G 460–64)

So the meaning of an 'ensumple' depends not on its content but on
the variable 'entente' of the people who use it. Alceste dismisses this
very Chaucerian argument rather impatiently ('Lat be thyn ar-
guynge'), and demands, as a 'penance', simply that Chaucer write
about women who, unlike Criseyde, were faithful in love. Thus she
dictates the content of the Legends, but leaves the poet free in the
critical matter of 'entente'.[88] Chaucer quite fairly makes the most

of this freedom, and produces a set of examples whose meaning, like that of the *Nun's Priest's Tale*, is extremely elusive and equivocal. Even the opening paragraph of his poem, with its unexceptionable sentiments about believing old books 'there as there is non other assay by preve', turns out, once it is recapitulated at ll. 81–8 (G-version) as an introduction to the legends themselves, to be a booby-trap. If all these legends come out of old books, as they do, does that not imply that there *is* 'non other assay by preve'? Perhaps Alceste, like the Clerk's Griselda, is not to be looked for nowadays, in the court of Richard II.[89]

The sophistication of the *Legend of Good Women* is quite appropriate in a work originally intended, it would seem, for presentation to Queen Anne 'at Eltham or at Sheene' (F 497). Here and elsewhere, Chaucer finesses upon the clerical traditions of the *exemplum*, producing results more subtle, and also more secular, than his contemporaries. Yet Gower and the *Gawain* poet and Langland all bring their own kinds of finesse to the old didactic mode, challenging both the intelligence and the imagination of readers. They work within the mode not as preachers but as poets.

V

In conclusion, let me summarize the main propositions put forward in this chapter.

The basic unit of Ricardian narrative is the single episode, not the cycle or series. The episode tends to have some clear exemplary significance, usually but not always endorsed by the author. The episode may be narrated at length or briefly; but whatever its scale, it will be set within some strongly-marked 'enclosing' form. A poem may consist of one such episode or several. In the latter case, the units may be related co-ordinately (as the Canterbury tales to each other) or subordinately (as Chauntecleer's stories of prophetic dreaming to the *Nun's Priest's Tale*); but in any case, the effect is not, except in *Purity*, rambling or 'Gothic'. The structures, like the narrative techniques and the significations, are clearly and deliberately articulated. The poets display a literary art which runs, in places, to mannerism and virtuosity; yet their sophistication does not impair the pristine energies of the story-telling. Unlike their contemporaries in France and Italy, they are above all story-tellers.

Chapter three

An Image of Man

The notion of a Ricardian 'image of man', proposed by the title of this chapter, is open to objection from two opposite quarters. It may be objected that English people of the later fourteenth century held no distinctively 'Ricardian' opinions about man: that their view of themselves and their place in the universal scheme was simply the time-honoured medieval view, and that there is, consequently, nothing to say about their 'image of man' which has not already been said for the whole of Western Christendom in the many general studies in the history of ideas. Others may object that the four poets discussed in this book differed so much in background and in temperament one from another that no useful purpose is served by trying to press them all into the service of a single vision.

However, my concern here will not be with people, not even with poets, but with poems. The poems of a given period generally resemble each other more than did the minds of the men who wrote them. They also differ more from the poems of other periods than appears from the 'world-view' which they offer for the inspection of historians. The image of man which such a group of poems forms (or may form) in the reader's mind is a complex, distinctive and essentially literary thing. It owes as much to prevailing conventions of poetic structure and conditions of poetic language as it does to the temper of authors or the opinions of an age. In what follows I shall try to suggest how, in poems of the Ricardian period, factors such as these combine to produce a common and characteristic 'image' of human life which is not only recognizably medieval but also recognizably Ricardian.

I

In his *Preface to Chaucer*, Professor D. W. Robertson notes the 'lack of anything approaching "heroic" suggestiveness' in the paintings of the Bohun MSS.[1] He also makes a more general observation: 'During the second half of the fourteenth century English art fails to show any outward manifestations of the heroic.'[2] This lack of heroic quality, he suggests, is also characteristic of the poetry of Chaucer: 'The English of Chaucer's day were not inspired by posturing in the grand manner, and in this matter Chaucer seems to have shared their taste.'[3] We may not wish to accept the reductive implication that all grand manner is merely 'posturing'; but I believe that the statement is in all essentials true, and of the first importance for the understanding not only of Chaucer but also of his literary contemporaries. The poems of the Ricardian period project an unheroic image of man. *Sir Gawain* and *Troilus*, as well as the *Canterbury Tales*, *Confessio Amantis* and *Piers Plowman*, lack 'heroic suggestiveness'. So does much other medieval poetry, of course; but it is possible to approach a definition of the distinctively Ricardian image by asking just why and in what ways it falls short of heroic stature. Such will be the method adopted in this chapter.

In my comparison between Chaucer's *Knight's Tale* and Boccaccio's *Teseida* in the last chapter, I pointed out that Chaucer's Knight shows relatively little interest in the heroic feats of arms which figure so prominently in Boccaccio's epic of love and war; and I suggested that this lack of interest in fighting was typical of Ricardian poetry generally. Troilus, Gawain and Theseus are warriors; but they fight offstage, and their prowess contributes little to our interest in them. We see them chiefly in their weeds of peace – Troilus within the walls of Troy, Gawain at Camelot and at Haut-desert, Theseus in Athens – living the civilian phase of their lives and much in the company of women. And there are, needless to say, few warrior-maids among the women. Chaucer makes no attempt to remind us in the *Knight's Tale* that Emily, like Hippolyta, is an Amazon with only one breast, the other having been removed for greater ease in the handling of a bow;[4] and when Cleopatra, in the *Legend of Good Women*, flees from the battle of Actium, he comments simply: 'No wonder was she myghte it nat endure' (656). The only notable case of a warrior-maid in Chaucer is Zenobia of Palmyrene, the doughty heroine of one of the Monk's tragedies (vii. 2247ff.) drawn from Boccaccio's *De Claris Mulieribus*.[5] Women play an exceedingly important part in Chaucer's poetry, as they do also in Gower's and in *Sir Gawain* and *Pearl*, but not as Amazons or

Valkyries. There is no Penthesilea or Camilla or Brunhilde or Britomart in the poetry of this period. The women are like Criseyde, womanish:

> She nas nat with the leste of hire stature,
> But alle hire lymes so wel answerynge
> Weren to wommanhod, that creature
> Was nevere lasse mannyssh in semynge   (i. 281–84)

and they exercise their authority in the chamber, not on the battle-field. This Ricardian lack of interest in fighting, and especially the civilian or 'chamber' quality which we find in the works of Chaucer, Gower and the *Gawain* poet, serves to distinguish the best poetry of this period in England both from the heroic poetry of the Anglo-Saxons and from Middle English minstrel romance. It also, as I suggested in the last chapter, sets this poetry apart from the main-stream of Renaissance narrative poetry both in England and else-where, insofar as Renaissance poets followed classical precedent in cultivating the 'matter of Mars'. When Spenser at the beginning of the *Faerie Queene* declares his intention 'for trumpets sterne to chaunge mine oaten reeds' and sing of 'fierce warres and faithful loves', he expresses a neo-classical ambition of which there is no trace in our period. The trumpet is not, poetically speaking, a Ricardian instrument.

In heroic poetry, whether Classical, Germanic or Renaissance, feats of arms are not normally performed or portrayed for their own sakes. They are interesting because they may decide the fates of kingdoms. In epic poetry, one critic has written, 'action is most fully realized through changes of institutions or regimes, changes which extend its consequences throughout society and throughout time. Thus the epic is the great poem of beginnings and endings. The *Aeneid* is typical, beginning with an ending and ending with a be-ginning.'[6] Here again Ricardian poetry stands quite outside epic traditions, for the actions with which it is concerned have no such momentous consequences. In the first stanza of *Sir Gawain* the poet recapitulates the great matters of Virgil's epic, the ending of Troy and the beginning of Rome; and he goes on to speak of another beginning – the founding of Britain by Felix Brutus, descendant of Aeneas and ancestor of Arthur. But whereas in *Beowulf* the genea-logical prologue of the Danish kings serves to introduce a hero who, both by his rank and by the historic (or pseudo-historic) significance of his battles, himself deserves to stand beside Scyld, Heremod and the other 'þeodcyningas', the corresponding prologue in *Gawain* introduces an adventure which has no significance at all for the history of the kings of Britain. Gawain's Adventure of the Green Chapel is just one of the 'outtrage awentures of Arthurez wonderez'. Some critics, it is true, have been tempted to see some connection between the adventure and the tragic end of Arthur and his Round Table.[7] But the poem does not, in Greene's phrase, 'extend the consequences' of its action in any such way. The reputation of the Round Table is perhaps at stake, but not the fate of the Kingdom.

Ricardian poets tend to centre their poems outside the great ages of 'beginnings and endings' towards which epic poets look. In *Piers Plowman* and *Confessio Amantis*, the present time of the poem is placed, in an explicit scheme of world history, at many removes from the ages of great founders and conquerors. Gower's Prologue concludes with the exposition of Nebuchadnezzar's dream of the golden image with feet of steel and earth. According to this, the great empires of Babylon (gold), Persia (silver), Greece (brass) and Rome (steel) have given place in modern times to the ignoble Holy Roman Empire (steel and earth). Thus the image

> Betokneth how the world schal change
> And waxe lasse worth and lasse,
> Til it to noght al overpasse . . .   (Prol. 628–30)

It introduces us to the unheroic latterday world in which Amans, as he says at the beginning of Book i, has to be content to live:

> I may noght strecche up to the hevene
> Min hand, ne setten al in evene
> This world, which evere is in balance:
> It stant noght in my sufficance
> So grete thinges to compasse . . .   (i. 1–5)

Later this wilful, even complacent unheroism of Amans is expressed in the Latin couplet:

> Non ego Sampsonis vires, non Herculis arma
> Vinco, sum sed ut hii victus amore pari.[8]

The rhetoric anticipates Prufrock: 'I am not Prince Hamlet, nor was meant to be.' In Langland's *Piers Plowman*, the historical perspective does not open until the latter part of the poem. In the *Do*

Bet section, we see Christ as knight, king and conqueror, triumphing over Satan and Death. This is a heroic victory whose consequence, portrayed at the beginning of *Do Best*, is the founding of the Catholic Church. There follows, in the remainder of the poem, a vision of the history of that Church from the time of Christ's Ascension up to the time in which Will himself lives. The Church grows 'lasse worth and lasse' until, in Will's day, it is on the point of succumbing to the attacks of Pride and Antichrist. This conflict between Antichrist and the Church might itself have provided Langland with a grand heroic ending, a tragic or triumphant eschatological finale; but he does not handle it in that way. Piers Plowman, the hero of the poem, is absent from the battle; Antichrist is a shadowy figure, and Will plays no part except to suffer at the hands of Elde a number of peculiarly humiliating physical injuries – baldness, loss of teeth, gout and sexual incapacity. The last and most dangerous episode in the siege is deliberately quiet and undramatic. A hypocritical friar, Friar Flatterer, gains admittance as a surgeon, and, once in, he lulls Contrition to sleep by his 'easy absolution':

> The Frere with his phisik this folke hath enchaunted,
> And plastred hem so esyly thei drede no synne . . .
>
> (xx. 376–7)

The age of persecutors has given place to an age of hypocrites, in which the heroic virtues of courage and physical endurance no longer have any meaning.

In the poetry of Chaucer, too, we find a pervasive sense of the unheroic, latterday character of contemporary realities. Typical is the Clerk's address to his fellow pilgrims at the end of his tale of Griselda:

> But o word, lordynges, herkneth er I go:
> It were ful hard to fynde now-a-dayes
> In al a toun Grisildis thre or two;
> For if that they were put to swiche assayes,
> The gold of hem hath now so badde alayes
> With bras, that thogh the coyne be fair at ye,
> It wolde rather breste a-two than plye.   (iv. 1163–9)

Chaucer's relationship, as a poet of 'now-a-dayes', to the epic poets and the great things they write about can be inferred from the

97

description of Fame's hall in the *House of Fame*. Although all nine Muses sing before Fame's throne, the only one mentioned by name is the 'mighty Muse' of epic poetry:

> So song the myghty Muse, she
> That cleped ys Caliope,
> And hir eighte sustren eke,
> That in her face semen meke;
> And ever mo, eternally,
> They songe of Fame . . .   (1399–1404)

Most of the pillars in the hall, accordingly, are of iron, 'Martes metal' (1446); and on them stand the epic poets of antiquity: Statius, bearing up the fame of Thebes; Homer, bearing up Troy; Virgil, bearing up Aeneas; Lucan, bearing up Caesar and Pompey. But the dreamer, the studious and unadventurous poet Geoffrey who has been carried up here by the Eagle, can do no more than wander among these pillars, staring up at their august occupants. Statius, standing on his iron pillar painted with tiger's blood, represents a kind of poetry to which he cannot aspire. He himself is a poet of Love, like Ovid, who stands here on a pillar of copper, Venus' metal; and even Ovid towers so far above Geoffrey as to be almost beyond his comprehension: 'also hye / As I myghte see hyt with myn ye' (1491–2). Like the rest of Chaucer's narrators, 'Geoffrey' is a dramatis persona; but his relationship to the epic poets in Fame's hall seems not unlike that of his creator. Virgil, Statius and 'Homer' (i.e. the writers who bore up the fame of Troy in the Middle Ages) are all major sources for Chaucer; but in every case the iron which they provide is used to fashion the setting for a love story – just such a story as 'Geoffrey' might have written 'in reverence / Of Love, and of hys servantes eke' (624–5). In the *House of Fame* itself the story of the *Aeneid* is recapitulated, but only because it figured on a wall in the Temple of Venus. The emphasis in the summary, accordingly, is on the unhappy love of Dido; and Aeneas gets little credit for his heroic destiny to found Rome. Despite a grudging mention of Mercury and his message, Aeneas is represented as a false lover, just as he is in the poem which the *House of Fame* here anticipates, the *Legend of Good Women*.[9] In the *Legend* the treatment of Aeneas is so very one-sided (the poet even suggests that Mercury's visit may have been a convenient fiction, 1295 ff.) that it drew a protest from Gavin Douglas, the Scottish translator of Virgil. In

calling Aeneas a false lover, says Douglas, Chaucer ignores Virgil's
plain intention to 'praise and magnify' the ancestor of Augustus:

> Bot sikkyrly of resson me behufis
> Excuss Chauser fra all maner repruffis:
> In lovyng of thir ladeis lylly-quhite
> He set on Virgill and Eneas this wyte,
> For he was evir (God wait) all womanis frend.[10]

No doubt Douglas misses some of the point of the *Legend* here; but
it is not only in the *Legend* that Chaucer's handling of epic materials
seems designed to please 'these ladies lily-white'. In *Anelida and
Arcite* (so far as we have it) Statius provides little more than the
background for another story of male treachery in love, so that the
stirring invocation to the 'ferse god of armes, Mars the rede' appears
quite incongruous. In the *Knight's Tale*, too, iron and tiger's blood
are subordinated to a romantic love-story, the fate of Thebes to the
fortunes of Palamon and Arcite. And in *Troilus* the Homeric matter
of the siege of Troy, though more richly developed by Chaucer than
by Boccaccio, takes second place to the 'double sorwe of Troilus . . .
in lovynge how his aventures fellen'.

The figure of Chaucer's Troilus illustrates how even the most
eligible Ricardian hero can fall short of epic stature. Troilus lives
in a great age of 'beginnings and endings', the era of the siege of
Troy; and as one of the sons of King Priam, he plays a prominent
part in the defence of the city. We see him both on the battleground
and in the council hall. As a warrior he is, we are told, second only to
Hector among the Trojans; and as a councillor he is present at the
parliament which Priam summons in Book iv. Like the hero of *Sir
Gawain*, he is one of the great ones. Yet his 'adventures in loving'
have even less public consequence than Gawain's Adventure of
the Green Chapel. They might have affected the outcome of the
siege if he had spoken up at Priam's council, like Hector, against
the exchange of prisoners; for if Criseyde had not been exchanged
for Antenor, the latter, as Chaucer reminds us (iv. 202 ff.), would
not have had the opportunity to betray Troy. But Troilus keeps
silent, for his own good reasons; and his love therefore remains a
secret known only to Criseyde and Pandarus, affected by the great
events of the siege but not affecting them. In this way it differs
from the love of Achilles for Patroclus which has such momentous
consequences in the *Iliad*, and also from the love of Dido which

could have distracted Aeneas from his great mission in the *Aeneid*. The main business of *Troilus*, like that of *Sir Gawain* and *Confessio Amantis*, is conducted in the chamber in the company of 'ladies lily-white', not on the battlefield or in the council hall. It is private business. Towards the end of his poem Chaucer commands it to 'kis the steppes, where as thow seest pace / Virgile, Ovide, Omer, Lucan, and Stace' (v. 1791–2); but any suggestion of epic ambition in this list has already been belied, three stanzas earlier, by Chaucer's address to his audience (of which I quoted part in the last chapter):

> And if I hadde ytaken for to write
> The armes of this ilke worthi man,
> Than wolde ich of his batailles endite;
> But for that I to writen first bigan
> Of his love, I have seyd as I kan, –
> His worthi dedes, whoso list hem heere,
> Rede Dares, he kan telle hem alle ifeere –
>
> Bysechyng every lady bright of hewe,
> And every gentil womman, what she be,
> That al be that Criseyde was untrewe,
> That for that gilt she be nat wroth with me . . .
>
> (v. 1765–75)

This is nearer to the chamber-music of the *Legend of Good Women* than to the trumpets of Homer or Statius, and it bears out D. S. Brewer's conclusion about Chaucer: 'Although he pays due respect to the public acts of his chivalric characters he is much more interested in their private and personal relationships and feelings, especially those to do with love.'[11]

The chief characters in Ricardian narrative, then, achieve little of public consequence. Their achievements are of the private, even questionable, kind which will not concern the historian. Hence the muted note on which *Troilus* ends – 'despitously' slain by Achilles and accorded no grand funeral that we hear of. Hence, too, the 'return to the starting point' which we noticed at the end of other Ricardian poems in considering structural circularity in the last chapter. Where epic moves forward to a triumphant or tragic close in which the achievements of the hero are celebrated, these poems turn back towards their starting place and reach there a muted and often doubtful conclusion. In the *Book of the Duchess*, the *Parliament of Fowls, Pearl* and *Piers Plowman*, the dreamer wakes up. Octavian, in the *Book of the Duchess*, returns to his castle; Gawain returns to Camelot; Gower's Amans returns home; and the Canterbury pilgrims would have returned to Southwark. Whatever achievement there may be seems a matter, not of changing the world by founding kingdoms or conquering enemies ('It stant noght in my sufficance / So grete thinges to compasse'), but of coming to terms with everyday realities and better understanding one's own nature and that of the world around one. The achievement, such as it is, is private and quotidian, rather than public and for all time. Thus the self-awareness which the hero achieves at the end of *Sir Gawain* does not seem secure for the future. It is not, and could hardly be, a permanent possession. It can only be preserved by the continual repetition, either in fact or through meditative recollection, of adventures such as that of the Green Chapel.[12] In this way the ending of *Sir Gawain* has something in common with that of *Piers Plowman*, where Conscience sets out once more in search of Piers. Both have a share in the spirit of Ecclesiasticus: 'When a man hath done, then he beginneth; and when he leaveth off, then shall he be doubtful.'

In Ricardian poetry generally, and especially in *Gawain* and *Piers*, this unheroic sense of the cyclic and repetitious character of human experience is associated with the cycle of the seasons of the year. In a powerful passage in *Purity*, God promises Noah that the catastrophe of the Flood will not be repeated:

> Sesounez schal yow never sese of sede ne of hervest,
> Ne hete, ne no harde forst, umbre ne droghthe,
> Ne the swetnesse of somer, ne the sadde wynter,
> Ne the nyght, ne the day, ne the newe yerez,
> Bot ever renne restlez – rengnez ye therinne!   (523–7)

The 'restless' running of the seasons is described again in a well-known passage at the beginning of the second fitt of *Sir Gawain*. The hero's adventure in this poem occupies a single year, from New Year's Day to New Year's Day, ending on the same day on which it began with a suggestion of unending, 'restless' repetition. In the linear time of history an achievement may appear final; but the cycle of the seasons makes us think of change and repetition, and therefore of the limits of human endeavour. The same poetic logic is at work in Passus vi of *Piers*. The episode of the half-acre, which occupies this passus, is important in the *Visio* as representing what the corrupt society of Lady Mede and the Seven Deadly Sins might become, if only people would repent and determine to 'do well' or live the life of 'truth'. This is a new order of things, presided over by Piers Plowman; and Piers, in Langland's poem, is always associated with the realization of full human potentialities for good. Yet Passus vi does not, in fact, represent anything like a Utopia. The people have listened to reason, repented and submitted to Piers; but they are still faced with the business of everyday living 'from Michaelmas to Michaelmas' (the phrase occurs at xiii. 240). The cycle of the year imposes, as it turns out, strict limitations on what Piers can achieve. At first all seems well. The people help Piers (it is autumn, or Michaelmas) with the plowing and preparing of the winter cornfield. But some people, the 'wasters', instead of working are idling and drinking; and Piers threatens to stop supplying them with food, calling upon the Knight to keep them in order. But it is only when Hunger appears and 'wrings their wombs' that they spring back to work. Hunger prevails throughout the winter and spring until Lammas (1 August), and at last 'newe corne cam to chepynge' (301). But then, as Piers had anticipated (207–9), the departure of Hunger leaves him back where he started; and the passus ends with the 'wasters' once more enjoying the abundance of the harvest. 'When a man hath done, then he beginneth.'

The life of the half-acre, properly lived, carries with it the promise of salvation, or at least the hope held out by Truth's pardon *(Qui bona egerunt, ibunt in vitam eternam)*; and the salvation of the soul is Langland's ultimate concern. Yet the life of the half-acre is also, considered as a social experiment, a failure. Even Piers, whose credentials as a faithful servant of Truth are beyond reproach, can achieve very little. His good society is based on fear and disintegrates as soon as the fear is removed. The frustration and failure which attend Piers's efforts to found a city of God on earth mark one of the limits, in Ricardian poetry, of human achievement.

II

In his essay '*Patience* and the *Gawain*-Poet', A. C. Spearing outlines the 'picture of life' presented by the four poems of the *Gawain* MS. as follows:

Man is placed in the context of an all-encompassing power, and
to defeat or outwit it he struggles absurdly and in vain. Thus
the hero becomes a hero *manqué*, a would-be hero. The heroic
or tragic aspiration is everywhere thwarted, and the heroic
conception of man is undercut and presented ironically. The
human 'hero' – now a hero only formally – in each of these
four poems is presented with sympathetic insight, with a full
and utterly convincing knowledge of thought and feeling, but
this knowledge is knowledge eventually of weakness.[13]

Dr Spearing observes that *Gawain, Pearl, Patience* and parts of
Purity all deal with a same situation: 'a confrontation between a
human being and some more than human power'.[14] It is, he suggests,
through these 'confrontations' that the poet articulates his sense of
man's thwarted heroism. Thus Jonah confronts God in *Patience*, the
dreamer confronts his transfigured Pearl in *Pearl*, and Gawain confronts the magisterial Green Knight in *Sir Gawain*. In each case the
protagonist is to some degree humbled by the confrontation, being
exposed in his human weakness.[15]

It seems to me that this idea of a humbling confrontation with
some 'more than human' or 'all-encompassing' power throws light
on the unheroic temper of Ricardian poetry generally, not just on
the poems of the *Gawain* MS. There are three well-known places in
Chaucer's work, for example, where the poet 'confronts' his protagonist with the immensity of the heavens: the space-flight in the
House of Fame, the summary of the *Somnium Scipionis* towards the
beginning of the *Parliament of Fowls*, and the flight of Troilus's soul
after his death at the end of *Troilus and Criseyde*. The significance of
such cosmic visions, so far as they concern the human observer, is
definitively stated by Boethius:

> Certeyn thyng is, as thou hast leerned by the demonstracioun
> of astronomye, that al the envyrounynge of the erthe aboute ne
> halt but the resoun of a prykke at regard of the gretnesse of
> hevene . . . And ye thanne, that ben envyrouned and closed
> withynne the leeste prykke of thilke prykke, thynken ye to
> manyfesten or publisschen your renoun and doon yowr name
> for to be born forth?[16]

This question casts its shadow, in Chaucer's poetry, across warriors,
lovers and poets alike. The vision of man 'envyrouned and closed'

within the least part of a world itself no more than a pinpoint receives ultimate expression in what many regard as the most characteristic of Chaucer's poems, the *Nun's Priest's Tale*. Here Chauntecleer, 'enclosed al aboute' in his little yard (a prick of a prick of a prick . . .) and loomed over by his mistress, the poor country widow, presents an image of insignificance in which the human reader is nevertheless forced to recognize himself.

In *Piers Plowman*, confrontations with august allegorical persons serve to chasten the protagonist. In Passus xi, for example, at the end of a rather nightmarish dream-within-a-dream, Will is conducted by Kynde (Chaucer's 'noble goddesse Nature') to a mountain, from which he can see 'the wondres of this worlde' spread out before him. He marvels at Nature's works:

> Briddes I bihelde that in buskes made nestes;
> Hadde nevere wye witte to worche the leest.
> I hadde wonder at whom and where the pye lerned
> To legge the stykkes in whiche she leyeth and bredeth;
> There nys wrighte as I wene shulde worche hir neste to paye;
> If any masoun made a molde therto moche wonder it were.
>
> (xi. 336–41)

Even a bird's nest is humbling to man, since no craftsman could match it. In what follows, Will is moved to angry protest and asks Reason (representing what is distinctively human in the nature of man) why man alone of all creatures behaves unreasonably. Reason's answer is chastening:

> man was made of suche a matere he may nought wel astert
> That ne some tymes hym bitit to folwen his kynde;
> Catoun acordeth therewith, *nemo sine crimine vivit* . . .
>
> (xi. 392–4)

'No man lives without sin': Reason's answer makes Will so ashamed that he wakes up.

Piers Plowman is a religious poem, and it is not surprising that Will's encounters with Nature and Reason (as well as Holy Church, Patience, Study and the rest) should serve to humble him. But even in a more secular, courtly piece like *Confessio Amantis* the allegorical persons have a magnitude and majesty as representatives of the order of God's creation. Consider the confrontation between Amans and Venus at the end of the poem Gower's Venus is not the disreputable figure of Chaucer's *Parliament of Fowls*. She is a noble goddess, representative of the divine order as it specially concerns Amans. The manner of their confrontation is, on both sides, very characteristic. When Venus first reappears, after the conclusion of Amans' confession and the presenting of his supplication, Amans falls upon his knee (viii. 2316) and prays for her grace; and later he again kneels (2900) when taking his leave of her. Kneeling is a specially common attitude in the literature and art of this period. King Richard himself kneels before the Virgin and Child in the Wilton Diptych. In the diptych, as in *Confessio Amantis* and in *Piers Plowman* (e.g. xix. 12), the humility of the gesture is graceful and affecting. In Chaucer, as so often, the humility may be touched with a suggestion of irony: the dreamer who kneels by the daisy in the Prologue to the *Legend of Good Women* bears an unmistakable affinity to the 'elvish' pilgrim Geoffrey staring at the ground in the *Canterbury Tales*.[17] But in Gower the effect is grave. Kneeling before Venus and gazing into her mirror, Amans learns to be old. The medical details are, as we should expect, less drastic here than in Langland's passage on the old age of Will; but the result is equally chastening. As Will retires into Unity (the Church), so Amans makes his 'beau retret' from the court of Venus and goes 'ther vertu moral duelleth' (viii. 2924–5). Venus, for her part, treats Amans firmly, even with a trace of scorn, but also humorously. At the beginning of the encounter she asks Gower his name 'as it were halvinge a game' (2319), and her parting advice to Amans, now healed of his love, is delivered laughingly:

> Venus behield me than and lowh,
> And axeth, as it were in game,
> What love was. And I for schame
> Ne wiste what I scholde ansuere;
> And natheles I gan to swere
> That be my trouthe I knew him noght;
> So ferr it was out of mi thoght,
> Riht as it hadde nevere be.
> 'Mi goode sone,' tho quod sche,
> 'Now at this time I lieve it wel,
> So goth the fortune of my whiel;
> Forthi mi conseil is thou leve' . . .   (viii. 2870–81)

This may remind us of Bertilak's laughing treatment of Gawain at the Green Chapel. Speaking of the 'supernatural power' represented by Bertilak and other similar figures in the poems of the *Gawain* MS., Spearing writes: 'It is a merciful power, and one that forgives human weakness; and it is precisely this that makes it so destructive of human dignity.'[18] Something the same might be said of Gower's Venus.

Another kind of 'confrontation', very prominent in Ricardian poetry and specially characteristic of the late medieval period, is that between penitent and confessor. The Fourth Lateran Council of 1215-16 had decreed that everyone was to confess his sins to his own priest at least once a year; and the immediate result of this canon *(Omnis utriusque sexus)* was greatly to increase the importance of the Sacrament of Penance in the later medieval church.[19] It is not surprising, therefore, that this sacrament should play an important part in the work of all four poets under discussion here. The *Canterbury Tales*, as we have it, ends with the *Parson's Tale*. This is sometimes spoken of rather vaguely as a 'sermon'; but it is in fact a formal treatise on the Sacrament of Penance, divided according to the three 'acts' of the sacrament: contrition, confession, satisfaction. The second part of the *Visio* of *Piers Plowman* is built around these same three 'acts';[20] and the confession of the Seven Deadly Sins to Repentance is one of the high points in the poem. In *Sir Gawain*, the hero's final encounter with his adversary at the Green Chapel culminates in a solemn, though non-canonical, act of confession. In *Confessio Amantis* the main device of the whole poem is, of course, the Lover's confession to Genius, priest and confessor of Venus. It will be evident that the confessors in Ricardian poetry are a somewhat motley crew – the Poor Parson, Repentance, Sir Bertilak, Genius. But they all serve, in their different ways, to confront the reader with a knowledge of human weakness formed in the confessional.

When Reason, in *Piers Plowman*, tells Will that 'No man lives without sin', his quotation from an elementary school-book (the *Distichs* of Cato) expresses an elementary truth. But this truth is not merely stated in the poems of our period; it is alive and active in them. Their moral psychology derives very largely from the 'psychology of sin' which had developed especially after the Fourth Lateran Council. One of the cardinal requirements of the Sacrament of Penance was that the penitent should make a full confession; and to do this he had to be able to identify by name the various sinful workings of his mind. The confessor could help him only if he was acquainted with some comprehensive scheme of moral psychology which, like a reference grid on a map, would enable them to cover all the ground together systematically. Scholastic moral philosophy, which was already well developed before 1215, was able to supply such schemes. There resulted, in the thirteenth and fourteenth centuries, a vigorous campaign to educate priests and people in the systematic understanding of themselves. The old idea of the Seven Deadly Sins, which had already been developed by scholastic thinkers into a much more complex and sophisticated scheme than Gregory ever dreamed of, provided the basic framework of this understanding. Innumerable treatises and manuals conveyed the skills of 'handling sin' to people who would otherwise have been far beyond the influence of the Schools.[21] The effects of this campaign can be traced in all the vernaculars of late medieval Europe. A treatise such as the *Summa Vitiorum*, written before 1250 by Guilielmus Peraldus, a Dominican and Doctor of the University of Paris, had a wide influence. The scheme of sins in Dante's *Purgatorio* appears to derive from this work, which is also the chief source of the *Manuel des Péchés*, from which in turn Robert Mannyng of Brunne derived his *Handlyng Synne*.[22] Peraldus also lies behind that lengthy section of Chaucer's *Parson's Tale* which is concerned with the Sins.[23] The title of this section conveys something of its character: 'Sequitur de septem peccatis mortalibus et eorum dependenciis, circumstanciis, et speciebus.'

Even before the Fourth Lateran Council, in the courtly literature of twelfth-century France, critics have recognized a connection between the practice of auricular confession (which was already spreading in that period) and a new taste for psychological analysis. One writer speaks of 'un approfondissement du sens de la faute'.[24] The results of this 'deepening' are very evident in Ricardian poetry. Gawain's confession to Bertilak at the Green Chapel, for example, clearly shows the influence of Peraldine moral psychology, and illustrates how this psychology tells against heroic pretensions. Gawain finds himself confronted with an adversary who, like God, sees his inmost secrets ('Now know I wel thy cosses, and thy costes als'); and the loss of that grand opacity which attracted at Hautdesert so many delightful compliments shocks Gawain into a confession which, although delivered to a layman, is represented as spiritually more significant than his confession to a priest at

Hautdesert the day before. Gawain's new sense of his own weakness, despite certain not unbecoming extravagances of expression ('Al fawty is my fare', for example), leads him to a view of human nature which is surely close to the poet's own: he speaks of

> The faut and the fayntyse of the flesche crabbed,
> How tender hit is to entyse teches of fylthe . . . (2435–6)

The wincing delicacy, close to revulsion, in these lines is Gawain's own; but the sense of the treacherousness ('fayntyse') of human nature and its susceptibility to sin is fully borne out by the poem. Like Hawkin in *Piers Plowman*, Gawain has been unable to preserve his baptismal innocence. The flesh seems actually to attract ('entyse') dirt to itself. As Hawkin says of his baptismal 'cote':

> couthe I nevere, by Cryste, kepen it clene an houre,
> That I ne soiled it with syghte or sum ydel speche,
> Or thorugh werke or thorugh worde, or wille of myn herte,
> That I ne flober it foule fro morwe tyl eve . . .   (xiv. 12–15)

Such generalizations are given substance, in *Sir Gawain*, by the hero's very exact and complete account of what went wrong in his own particular case at Hautdesert:

> For care of thy knokke cowardyse me taght
> To acorde me with covetyse, my kynde to forsake,
> That is larges and lewté that longez to knyghtez.
> Now am I fawty and falce, and ferde haf ben ever
> Of trecherye and untrawthe . . .   (2379–83)

In a passage like this the discipline of the confessional, and more remotely the moral psychology of the scholastics, bear literary fruit. The poet has available for Gawain a language which, though still poetic and metaphorical, is capable of 'handling sin' with formal precision, isolating the three components in Gawain's case, cowardice, covetousness, and untruth (cf. 2508–9), and identifying their interrelations. Cowardice in face of the Green Knight's blow leads to an act (the withholding of the girdle from the Host) which, objectively considered, is an act of covetousness prejudicing Gawain's knightly virtue of 'largess', but which is also – and more significantly – an act of untruth, a failure of loyalty towards the Host.[25] Such is Gawain's account of his case to his confessor.

In Gower's *Confessio Amantis*, too, the knowledge of the private workings – and, ultimately, the weakness – of human nature displayed in the poem owes much to the discipline of the confessional. The confrontation between Amans and his confessor Genius is not only a frame for the stories Genius tells. Each story is told to illustrate a particular sin or species of sin, or a corresponding virtue; and the reader's attention is thereby directed towards a specific aspect of the behaviour of the characters in the story, an aspect formally defined in terms of the scheme of the Seven Deadly Sins, 'their dependencies, circumstances, and species'. The drawback of this arrangement is that it tends to narrow our responses to a chosen episode. Even simple bits of behaviour can rarely be understood fully in terms of one single species of sin; and it is, in any event, the complicated case (like that of Gawain) which is most interesting. Complexities of character and motive do occur in the confessor's *exempla*; but they occur despite the formal scheme, not because of it. However, there is one character in the *Confessio* who is given the full treatment, and that is Amans himself. The confessor questions him about all the species of all the sins in the scheme: 'Art thou, mi sone, of such engin?', 'Hast thou supplanted eny man?', 'Hast thou be oon / Of hem that slowthe hath so begon?', and so on. Sometimes Amans answers 'yes' and sometimes 'no'; and there are so many of these answers that, like the black dots and blanks produced by a photo-engraver's screen, they combine to produce something like a complete shaded portrait, at least of Amans as a lover. The technique contrasts with the allegorical method by which Guillaume de Lorris, through the interaction of various personifications, builds up 'portraits' of lover and lady in the *Roman de la Rose*.[26] The result is less bold, more sober and 'photographic'.

At each of the confessor's questions, Amans is faced with a simple binary choice: he can either say 'yes' or 'no'. But his answer is commonly supported by an autobiographical passage in which he describes his behaviour so far as it is relevant to the point at issue. These passages usually bring out the best in Gower. In Book iv (the Book of Sloth), for example, Genius asks Amans whether he has been idle in love. Amans replies that, on the contrary, he has been busy, and goes on to describe how assiduously he has served his lady. One piece from this description has already been quoted as an example of Gower's style; but the whole passage (iv. 1122–1223) is masterly in its evocation of the lover's anxious attentions, his small pleasures and his not-too-desperate pains. This is '*voir dit*' at its best. But we must note that Amans produces his catalogue of lover's attentions in response to his confessor's question: 'What hast thou don of besischipe?'. The realistic details of courtly setting and amorous psychology are called up in the process of confessional inquiry ('opposing', as Gower calls it), and they remain strictly within its formal categories. And there is a further point. Genius, as Love's confessor, is pleased to hear how busy Amans has been in Love's service; but at the end of the poem, once the 'sotie' or foolishness of Amans has been revealed to him and to us, the reader is encouraged to see his confessions in a new light, as contributions to a portrait of weakness and folly. Amans, we learn, is old; and the old should have better things to do than dance attendance on ladies. Repose, not 'business', is their proper state. So Gower, using methods of confessional analysis, arrives finally at a judgment of Amans which even Chaucer's Parson might endorse.

I do not wish to suggest that all the characters in the various works of our four poets are submitted to the kind of psychological scrutiny cultivated in the confessional; nor that all of them turn out to be examples of 'the faut and the fayntyse of the flesche crabbed'. For one thing, although 'heroes' in the old manner are absent from Ricardian narrative, saints and saintly persons are not. It is enough to recall one group of heroines in the *Canterbury Tales*: the Nun's St Cecilia, the Man of Law's Constance, the Physician's Virginia, the Clerk's Griselda, Chaucer's Prudence. These figures, whose names all either speak of virtue (on 'Cecilia', see viii. 85 ff.) or, as in the case of Griselda, have come to do so, bear little trace of human weakness about them. They are all shining examples of the virtues of quiet steadfastness and longsuffering – virtues which represent, perhaps, the only kind of heroism viable in Chaucer's latter-day world. But these exemplary figures of hagiography and romance are remote from what we might call the 'real' world of the Canterbury pilgrimage. The Clerk says that true Griseldas are not to be found nowadays; and the Host, at the conclusion of *Melibee*, ruefully contrasts Prudence with his own wife, Goodelief. Goodelief and the Wife of Bath, with all the 'badde alayes' in their mettle, represent another extreme which is, however, nearer to the Ricardian norm. For the poems of this period are pervaded by a sense, not only of the littleness of human concerns, but also of the often unsuspected weakness and perversity of human nature. *Nemo sine crimine vivit.*

III

But Cato's maxim could not stand as the last word in this chapter. An awareness of sin formed in the severe discipline of the confessional does contribute to the unheroic image of man which these poems project; but the poems are not committed to any narrowly 'penitential' view of man. Their most intimate and pervasive quality, indeed, is a sense of humour; and this humour, even though it may itself be supported by the Catholic faith, as Chestertonian critics contend, yields a broad and unsectarian view of things, within which that faith can be contained and its severer manifestations 'placed'. This is the 'large, free, simple, clear yet kindly view of human life' which Arnold, himself no Christian, could yet appreciate in Chaucer, and which we may also find, I shall suggest, in the *Gawain* poet, Gower and Langland.

Medieval poets were in general quite ready to admit humorous turns of expression into solemn passages;[27] and it is not surprising that Ricardian poets, working in a vernacular which still preserved much of its homely and demotic character after centuries of relative neglect by polite authors, should have admitted them more readily than most. By comparison with their French contemporaries, these English poets do indeed – to adopt a phrase from Chaucer's mocking apology for his *Canterbury Tales* – 'speak full broad'. Their style includes a whole range of pithy, humorous, often proverbial expressions, such as may be sufficiently recalled by a single example from Langland. Holy Church says to Will:

But if ye loven lelliche and lene the poure,
Such goed as god yow sent godelich parteth,
Ye ne have na more meryte in masse ne in houres
Than Malkyn of hire maydenhode that no man desireth . . .

(i. 179–82)

This broad and humorous manner is no less characteristic of Ricardian verse than a correct and witty manner is of Augustan. Some works exhibit it more than others: *Piers* more than *Confessio Amantis*, *Patience* more than *Sir Gawain*; but even in the most narrowly courtly works, and against their grain, it makes its presence felt as a constituent in the style. What concerns us here is to see how this humorous manner contributes to the image of man in Ricardian poetry, and especially how the poets bring it to bear upon their 'heroes'.

I take as my chief illustration the scene in Chaucer's *Knight's Tale* in which Theseus, hunting outside Athens, comes upon the two young Theban heroes fighting in a grove for the love of Emily. Theseus first condemns them to death, but then, persuaded by the pleading of the ladies, he relents:

> Yet in his resoun he hem bothe excused,
> As thus: he thoghte wel that every man
> Wol helpe hymself in love, if that he kan,
> And eek delivere hymself out of prisoun . . . (i. 1766–9)

Then, looking up with 'eyen lighte', Theseus pronounces his great speech on the power of Cupid, beginning 'The god of love, a, *benedicite*', a speech which lies close to the centre, not only of Chaucer's achievement, but also of the whole achievement of the age. Love, says Theseus, has made Palamon and Arcite act against their vital interests by hanging around Athens and risking their lives:

> Now looketh, is nat that an heigh folye?
> Who may been a fool, but if he love?
> Bihoold, for Goddes sake that sit above,
> Se how they blede! be they noght wel arrayed?
> Thus hath hir lord, the god of love, ypayed
> Hir wages and hir fees for hir servyse!
> And yet they wenen for to been ful wyse
> That serven love, for aught that may bifalle.
> But this is yet the beste game of alle,
> That she for whom they han this jolitee
> Kan hem therfore as muche thank as me.
> She woot namoore of al this hoote fare,
> By God, than woot a cokkow or an hare!
> But all moot ben assayed, hoot and coold;
> A man moot ben a fool, or yong or oold, –
> I woot it by myself ful yore agon,
> For in my tyme a servant was I oon.
> And therefore, syn I knowe of loves peyne,
> And woot hou soore it kan a man distreyne,

As he that hath ben caught ofte in his laas,
I yow foryeve al hoolly this trespaas,
At requeste of the queene, that kneleth heere,
And eek of Emelye, my suster deere . . . (i. 1798–1820)

The 'breadth' of this style comes out best in comparison with Dryden's version in *Palamon and Arcite* (Book ii. 350 ff.), where much of the humour is lost in the 'polishing'. The lines beginning 'But this is yet the beste game of alle', for instance, are rendered by Dryden:

This is not all: the fair for whom they strove
Nor knew before, nor could suspect their love,
Nor thought, when she beheld the fight from far,
Her beauty was th' occasion of the war . . . (374–7)

In these elegant lines Theseus' challenge to the young lovers confines itself to the point at issue: if Emily *had* known of their love, we feel, Dryden's Theseus would have been satisfied. Chaucer's Theseus, on the other hand, uses language which, precisely where it must have struck Dryden as indecorous in a heroic poem ('she' instead of 'the fair', 'this hoote fare' instead of 'their love', and especially the comparisons with cuckoo and hare), challenges the very vision of Emily by which both Palamon and Arcite are inspired. Emily, Chaucer invites us to recall, is Theseus' sister-in-law; and this domestic relationship helps Theseus to see the romantic passion of the two young men from the outside. From this vantage-point he brings to bear upon them a teasing, bantering humour which leaves our own view of their case permanently modified. Not that their conduct is put beyond the range of a reader's sympathies; but they are far from imposing upon us their own view of their case. Their love is 'the loveris maladye of Hereos', rather than 'heroic love' in the Renaissance sense.[28] We are permitted to see its medical side, and also its funny side.

Theseus' treatment of Palamon and Arcite in this scene has a close parallel towards the end of *Sir Gawain* in Bertilak's treatment of Gawain at the Green Chapel. Here again a character of especial power and authority brings a teasing humour to bear on a hero in whose feelings and preoccupations he has no reason to share. Bertilak does not *feel* Gawain's mortification and sense of failure, any more than Theseus feels the jealous passion of Palamon and

Arcite. Just as Emily is simply a sister-in-law to Theseus, so Bertilak can represent Morgan la Faye, the cause of Gawain's current misery, in an equally mundane and domestic light: 'Ho is even thyn aunt, Arthurez half-suster'. But Bertilak's attitude of humorous, sympathetic detachment towards Gawain is best represented at the moment after his delivery of the return blow, when Gawain, his pledge now honoured, springs into an attitude of defence:

> The hathel heldet hym fro, and on his ax rested,
> Sette the schaft upon schore, and to the scharp lened,
> And loked to the leude that on the launde yede,
> How that doghty, dredles, dervely ther stondez
> Armed, ful aghlez: in hert hit hym lykez.
> Thenn he melez muryly wyth a much steven,
> And wyth a rynkande rurde he to the renk sayde:
> 'Bolde burne, on this bent be not so gryndel . . .'   (2331–8)

Gawain's reaction has been eminently natural. He is now at last freed from the obligation (especially onerous to a knight) of standing still to be hit; and he cannot know that there is no further danger to fear. His courage and quickness please the reader, as they please Bercilak. But at the same time Bertilak's strong, merry speech, almost fatherly in its calming humour, allows us to see a funny side to Gawain's 'gryndellayk'.[29]

In both Gower and Langland there is more humour than is commonly supposed. Gower's poetry certainly is, as Thomas Warton observed, 'of a grave and sententious turn';[30] but his treatment of Amans resolves, as we have seen, into a confrontation with Venus in which the goddess treats the lover in a laughing fashion which recalls Bertilak. Here as in the *Knight's Tale* the poet shows the 'sotie' or folly of amorous concerns; and although Gower gives the revelation a distinctly more moral turn than does Chaucer, his treatment of Amans remains basically humorous to the end. At the very end, in a passage quoted in the last chapter, Amans returns home smiling to himself and resolving to give up the lover's life. But why?

> whanne y sigh non othre weie
> Bot only that y was refusid,
> Unto the lif which y hadde usid
> I thoughte nevere torne ayein . . .   (viii. 2962–5)

The 'moral virtue' of Amans is forced upon him: smilingly, he 'makes a virtue of necessity'. And that maxim, cited by Theseus at the end of the *Knight's Tale* (3041–2), may suggest how Gower is still moving as much in the world of humorous awareness and acceptance of things as they are, as in the world of moral choices to which (inspired by Chaucer's epithet '*moral* Gower') we are inclined to confine him.

In his section on Langland in the *History of English Poetry*, Thomas Warton speaks more than once about the poet's 'humour'.[31] Insofar as this humour is directed outwards against corrupt judges and hypocritical friars (the clergy, says Warton, are 'ridiculed with much humour and spirit') it does not concern us here. But there is also a vein of 'Chaucerian' humour which some readers fail to see because they do not expect it – a retroflex humour, which turns back and plays upon the preoccupations of the poem itself. A striking instance of this is the waking interlude introduced in the C-text between the two dreams of the *Visio*.[32] This interlude acts as a prologue to the second of the dreams, in which Langland is to be concerned with 'Do Well' chiefly as it manifests itself in honest labour in the half-acre of human society. One hot harvest season, Will meets Reason and Conscience, the two characters who at the end of his first and latest dream had triumphed over Mede at Westminster. Reason 'opposes' him (the word used by Gower of his confessor's questionings), asking him why he is not at work in the harvest, or in some other honest occupation. There follows a subtle and amusing piece of dialogue in which Will tries to defend himself by arguing, first that he is too delicate and too tall for work in the fields, and then that as a 'clerk' he should not be asked to do 'knavish' work in any case. As he develops the latter point, one recognizes the argumentative manner which Langland uses often elsewhere in his poem: scornful complaint about the decay of contemporary society (bondmen's children have become bishops!) and excited piling up of scriptural authorities, culminating in a lofty conclusion:

> 'Preyers of a parfyt man and penaunce discret
> Ys the leveste labour that oure Lord pleseth.
> *Non de solo,*' ich seide, 'for sothe *vivit homo,*
> *Nec in pane et pabulo,* the *Paternoster* witnesseth:
> *Fiat voluntas tua* fynt ous alle thynges' ...　　(vi. 84–8)

Authentic Langland; but listen to what follows:

> Quath Conscience, 'by Crist, ich can nat see this lyeth;
> Ac it semeth nouht parfytnesse in cytees for to begge,
> Bote he be obediencer to pryour other to mynstre'.
>
> (vi. 89-91)

'I cannot see that this excuse is admissible.'[33] Will has spoken of
himself, by implication, as a 'perfect man'; but begging does not
seem, Conscience mildly observes, to be a perfect life – or not in
Will's circumstances.[34] The rebuke pierces Will's defensive rhetoric
and leads him to his beautiful acknowledgment of a wasted life. He
confesses his fault and expresses hope of amendment:

> So hope ich to have of hym that is almyghty
> A gobet of hus grace, and bygynne a tyme
> That alle tymes of my tyme to profit shal turne . . .
>
> (99–101)

But even the elevation and 'lift' of this is rhetorical; and the responses of Reason and Conscience, with which the interlude ends,
reawaken suspicions of Will's good faith:

> 'Ich rede the,' quath Reson tho, 'rape the to bygynne
> The lyf that ys lowable and leel to the soule' –
> 'Ye, and continue,' quath Conscience; and to the kirke ich wente.

'You speak of beginning', says Reason, 'so hurry up and begin'; to
which Conscience adds his characteristically dry and laconic comment. The effect of this interlude in the C-text is not to invalidate
the knowledge which comes to Will in his ensuing dream; but the
reader of the C-text can anticipate all the self-deceptions and
rationalizations by which dreamer and reader alike may succeed in
protecting themselves from the impact of that knowledge. Like
other protagonists in Ricardian poetry, Langland's Will is caught,
in the C-text, in a humorous cross-light. Hence the didactic business
of the dream is carried on in greater awareness of things as they are.

Perhaps it is part of the nature of humour (as against wit) to
entail some acceptance of 'things as they are'. Humour tends in all
periods to be clement and accommodating. But each period will
have its own terms of acceptance and grounds of accommodation.
To get an idea of what these are in the Ricardian period, let me
turn back first to Theseus' speech in the *Knight's Tale*. In the long

passage already quoted from this speech, Theseus gives two reasons
for his decision to forgive Palamon and Arcite: the intercession of
the royal ladies, and his own knowledge of what love is like. For he
himself has been a lover 'in his time':

> But all moot ben assayed, hoot and coold;
> A man moot ben a fool, or yong or oold, –
> I woot it by myself ful yore agon,
> For in my tyme a servant was I oon.   (i. 1811–14)

Theseus, as we have seen, is a mature, Jovian man, a governor and a
conqueror.[35] So far as his relations with women are concerned, he is
now (to use the Franklin's phrases, v. 793) more 'lord in mariage'
than 'servant in love'. But he recognizes that passionate love is inevitable and that youth is the time for it – for Palamon and Arcite,
as it once was for him. His recognition of their love, 'I woot it by
myself', seems to imply a happy, mutually respectful relationship
between the Knight (who treats Palamon and Arcite generously in
his story) and his son, the Squire, 'a lovere and a lusty bacheler'.
Theseus stands to Palamon and Arcite as the Knight stands to the
Squire; while beyond Theseus we perceive dimly the figure of his
father, the aged Egeus, whose point of view differs as much from
Theseus' as Theseus' does from that of the young lovers:

> This world nys but a thurghfare ful of wo,
> And we been pilgrymes, passynge to and fro.
> Deeth is an ende of every worldly soore . . . (i. 2847–9)

The saturnine wisdom of Egeus belongs – if we are to assign it to a
Canterbury pilgrim – not to the Knight but to the Parson.[36]

The general principle involved here is succinctly stated by the
Host, when he reproaches the Clerk for brooding on logical problems when everyone else is enjoying himself:

> But Salomon seith 'every thyng hath tyme.'
> For Goddes sake, as beth of bettre cheere!   (iv. 6–7)

So far as the course of an individual life is concerned, there follows
from this biblical maxim the doctrine of the Ages of Man – each age
with different activities and preoccupations appropriated to it. This
doctrine, important but implicit in the *Knight's Tale*, becomes explicit in *Confessio Amantis* when, towards the end of the poem, we
discover that Amans is old. When Chaucer's Theseus says 'A man

moot ben a fool, or yong or oold', he means, of course, that he should be a fool young.[37] The figure of the old fool, the *senex amans* who sins against the decorum of the ages of man, is traditionally an object of moral censure (as in Chaucer's *Merchant's Tale*) and of ridicule (as in the *Miller's Tale*); but Gower portrays the type with refreshing delicacy and humour. The delicacy springs from the fact that the reader does not know that Amans is old until towards the end. The reader can therefore respond to his account of his passion in a fresh, unprejudiced fashion; and this allows him to recognize in the end that an old man's love, though it can never *look* like a young man's, may very well *feel* like it. The humour springs from the doctrine of the Ages of Man. It is this doctrine which Venus finally invokes against the lover:

> For loves lust and lockes hore
> In chambre acorden neveremore . . . (viii. 2403-4)

Or, as the Latin verses put it:

> Conveniens igitur foret, ut quos cana senectus
> Attigit, ulterius corpora casta colant.[38]

So the lover looks in Venus' mirror and, seeing his wrinkles and grey hairs, makes a comparison or 'liknesse' between the course of his life and the twelve months of the year, each of which is different:

> For who the times wel recordeth,
> And thanne at Marche if he beginne,
> Whan that the lusti yeer comth inne,
> Til Augst be passed and Septembre,
> The myhty youthe he may remembre
> In which the yeer hath his deduit
> Of gras, of lef, of flour, of fruit,
> Of corn and of the wyny grape.
> And afterward the time is schape
> To frost, to snow, to wind, to rein,
> Til eft that Mars be come ayein:
> The wynter wol no somer knowe . . . (viii. 2842-53)

The comparison represents the lover's decision to give up love as natural and inevitable. He is no moral hero. He is reconciling himself to things as they inevitably are, making a virtue of necessity; and

the rueful, humorous and quite unfanatical tone of the whole ending
reflects this.

In Langland, too, a sense of an inevitable order in the unfolding
of individual experience yields this same humour – resigned and
muted, but unmistakable. Let me take an example from the end of
the dinner scene in Passus xiii. Conscience is giving a dinner at his
house with Clergy and a gluttonous Friar as chief guests, while Will
and the pilgrim Patience eat at a side-table. The conversation turns
to Dowel, and Patience speaks so eloquently on the subject that
Conscience suddenly decides on an impulse to go off, leaving his
own dinner party, to become a pilgrim in his company. Clergy expresses surprise at his behaviour, but Conscience persists:

> Thus curteislich Conscience congeyde fyrst the Frere,
> And sithen softliche he seyde in Clergyes ere,
> 'Me were lever, by owre lorde, and I lyve shulde,
> Have pacience perfitlich than half thi pakke of bokes!'
> Clergy to Conscience no congeye wolde take,
> But seide ful sobreliche, 'Thow shalt se the tyme
> Whan thow art wery for-walked wilne me to consaille'.
> 'That is soth,' seyde Conscience, 'so me God helpe!
> If Pacience be owre partyng-felawe and pryve with us bothe,
> There nys wo in this worlde that we ne shulde amende,
> And confourmen kynges to pees and al kynnes londes,
> Sarasenes and Surre and so forth alle the Iewes
> Turne into the trewe feithe and intil one byleve'.
> 'That is soth,' quod Clergye, 'I se what thow menest.
> I shal dwelle as I do, my devore to shewen,
> And conformen fauntekynes and other folke ylered,
> Tyl Pacience have preved the and parfite the maked' . . .
>
> (xiii. 198–214)

The enthusiasm of Conscience for the life of patience and the
possibilities of individual perfection and universal faith and brother-
hood which it holds out is admirable, especially when set beside the
complacency of the Friar. But the sober words of Clergy ('booklearning') serve to place this enthusiasm, and even to show up, unexpectedly, its funny side.[39] Conscience probably will need to fall
back on booklearning, once his fires of enthusiasm have burnt
down; and he may even, as Clergy's verbal echo suggests, some day
become content to 'conformen' (v.r. 'confermen' at l. 213) children

at the font instead of 'kynges to pees and al kynnes londes'. Clergy's dry humour has its source in a mature, or one might prefer to say 'middle-aged', sense of the limits of human achievement and the importance of dull, everyday duties. His attitude towards Conscience's youthful aspirations is almost that of Theseus towards the youthful passions of Palamon and Arcite. It embodies the moderate and moderating virtue which in Middle English was called 'mesure'.

The age of a character is only one of many variables by which attitude and behaviour are determined: others include sex, nationality, occupation (knight, miller . . .), current role or function (challenger, master of ceremonies, messenger . . .), season of the year, ecclesiastical season (advent, Christmas . . .), and even time of day. The differences of attitude and behaviour which such variables entail are fully displayed in Ricardian poetry. The poets seem to delight in showing how 'diversely' people behave and react in accordance with their different circumstances. In Chaucer and the *Gawain* poet, especially, this diversity is a prime source of humour.

The end of *Sir Gawain* seems to leave the reader with a problem similar to that raised in another 'lay', Chaucer's *Franklin's Tale*, where the Franklin asks his audience to decide which of his characters has acted most generously (v. 1621–2). For the alliterative poem ends on an unresolved disharmony concerning the gravity of Gawain's fault. One can imagine an audience left debating, in a half-serious mood of chamber casuistry, whose account to accept. Was Gawain, as he himself believes, gravely at fault? Or are Bertilak and the court right to treat his slip as a venial one? It is unlikely that such a discussion would ever reach a conclusion, however, since the original disagreement is of a peculiar kind. Everyone concerned knows not only what Gawain did but also why he did it: the hero's own analysis of the moral structure of the case is nowhere contradicted. The differences arise in the final assessment of the case, and have their source, not in any disagreement about facts, but in differences of circumstance and role. Gawain, the hero still engrossed in his adventure, is bound to take a serious view of his own case. Excuses would be untimely and indecorous (though he does attempt one in conversation with Bertilak, 2414–28). Precisely because Gawain fulfils so thoroughly, by his intense and evident mortification, the requirements of his role, Bertilak and later Arthur's court are free to play their own parts just as unreservedly. So the fair-minded adversary and the hero's companions unite in laughter, congratulations, and 'comfort'. Gawain does not take the comfort or accept the congratulations, still less join in the laughter; but in due time he may, just as 'by processe and by lengthe of certeyn yeres' Palamon and Emily come to the end of their period of mourning for Arcite. For as Theseus says on that occasion, 'al this thyng hath ende'. Read in this way, in accordance with the sense of times and seasons which we find everywhere in this period, the ending of *Gawain* appears less problematic than some critics would have it.

Modern critics are rather quick to find in medieval literature ideological conflicts in which one philosophy or tradition is played off against another. But very often the oppositions in question arise from the simple demands of differing role and circumstance, and have little or no ideological significance. Gawain does not, by virtue of his behaviour at the end of the poem, represent some tradition of Christian chivalry more severe and uncompromising than that re-presented by Bertilak or Arthur. Nor does the contrast in speech and behaviour between Troilus and Pandarus in Chaucer's *Troilus* reflect an opposition between 'bourgeois' and 'courtly' traditions.[40] Pandarus does not, like Troilus, have royal blood in his veins; but he moves in courtly circles, not bourgeois ones. The freedom of speech and action which he displays in his handling of Troilus' affair derives, not from bourgeois nature or principle, but from the fact that it is not his affair. In his own affair (what we see of it), he behaves much like Troilus, passing sleepless nights and remaining faithful despite the obduracy of his beloved. Where he is himself concerned, as Troilus points out in a spirited passage, his wisdom fails him:

> Thow koudest nevere in love thiselven wisse:
> How devel maistow brynge me to blisse?   (i. 622–3)

But Troilus' conclusion does not follow, as Pandarus is able to show; for in relation to Troilus' love his role is that of the friend, concerned but not engrossed by the affair, and in this role he can both think more coolly and (where occasion requires) speak more broadly than ever Troilus could – or should. The modality of cir-cumstance and role is very clearly evident here, since Pandarus (unlike Theseus) is himself currently a lover and might, in a dif-ferent poem, suffer the jocularities of Troilus. It was after all Troilus himself who, before he fell in love with Criseyde, used to make a point of chaffing lovers, very much in Pandarus' style:

God woot, she slepeth softe
For love of the, whan thow turnest ful ofte!   (i. 195–6)

By showing individuals in the company of other people whose
circumstances (rather than their personalities or their philosophies)
are different, Ricardian poets indulge their taste for bold contrasts
and humorous cross-lights. Just two individuals (Pandarus and
Troilus, Gawain and Bertilak) may be sufficient; but crowds are
also full of possibilities. None of these poets, I have suggested, shows
much interest in public affairs; great matters of state or city, the
matters of epic, lie outside their compass. But a *crowd*, a company of
'sondry folk' massed together and displaying – often to distinctly
comic effect – rich varieties of behaviour, opinion or attitude,
interests them very much, not as a political force but as a conglo-
merate of private persons. They call it a 'press' or, less often, a
'rout'. In minor examples, a crowd of bystanders (usually anonymous) gathers round a centre of interest and expresses opinions
(usually conflicting). The liveliest instance is in Chaucer's *Squire's
Tale*, where a 'press' swarms round the mysterious brass horse:

It was of Fairye, as the peple semed.
Diverse folk diversely they demed;
As many heddes, as manye wittes ther been.
They murmureden as dooth a swarm of been,
And maden skiles after hir fantasies . . .   (v. 201–5)

Similarly in the *Knight's Tale*, on the morning of the great tournament, the palace is 'ful of divynynge':

Somme seyden thus, somme seyde 'it shal be so';
Somme helden with hym with the blake berd,
Somme with the balled . . .   (i. 2516–18)

In *Sir Gawain*, too, we hear the 'divining' of anonymous onlookers:
at the moment of Gawain's departure from Camelot ('Bi Kryst, hit
is scathe / That thou, leude, schal be lost, that art of lyf noble',
674–5), and on his arrival at Hautdesert ('Now schal we semlych se
sleghtez of thewez / And the teccheles termes of talkyng noble',
916–17). Even Gower's Amans, who spends most of the poem
closeted with Genius, does not escape from the press. After receiving
Venus' advice to relinquish love, Amans falls into a swoon in which

he sees Cupid accompanied by 'sondri routes' ('variis turmis' in the side-note) of lovers, old and young, who crowd round his prostrate body:

> And, as me thoghte, anon ther was
> On every side so gret presse,
> That every lif began to presse,
> I wot noght wel hou many score . . .
>
> (viii. 2750–3)

They discuss his case:

> Tho myhte I hiere gret partie
> Spekende, and ech his oghne avis
> Hath told, on that, an other this . . .   (2760–2)

Some say that an old man has no excuse for falling in love, others that love attacks men of all ages:

> And thus me thoghte, in sondri place
> Of hem that walken up and doun
> Ther was diverse opinioun . . .   (2780–2)

The diversity of opinion represented by the 'press' in these courtly poems is naturally rather limited. Elsewhere in Ricardian narrative one finds more motley crowds and broader, more demotic effects. Langland's field full of folk is the arena in which both the dreams of the *Visio* take place; and the sense of the crowded variety of humanity which he conveys so vividly in the Prologue stays with the reader to the end of the poem:

> alle maner of men, the mene and the riche,
> Worchyng and wandryng as the worlde asketh . . .
>
> (Prol. 18–19)

But the greatest master of the crowded canvas in this period is, of course, Chaucer. He starts in the *House of Fame* with the 'companies' or 'routs' which enter the temple of Fame and make their various requests to the goddess. Here the varieties of human desire and fortune are represented schematically: there are those who deserve and want fame and get it, those who deserve and get it but do not want it, etc. But the companies are genuine crowds, not squads:

> I herde a noyse aprochen blyve,
> That ferde as been don in an hive

> Ayen her tyme of out-fleynge . . .
> . . . ther come entryng into the halle
> A rhyght gret companye withalle,
> And that of sondry regiouns,
> Of alleskynnes condiciouns
> That dwelle in erthe under the mone,
> Pore and ryche.   (1521–32)

The same swarming effect is created later in the poem, when a 'congregacioun of folk', massed together in the wicker house of Rumour, keeps up a continuous hum of gossip and 'opinioun':

> 'Nost not thou
> That ys betyd, lo, late or now?'
> 'No,' quod he, 'telle me what.'
> And than he tolde hym this and that,
> And swor therto that hit was soth –
> 'Thus hath he sayd,' and 'Thus he doth'.   (2047–52)

Like the house of Rumour, the lawn where Nature holds her meeting in the *Parliament of Fowls* is so crowded that the narrator can hardly find a spot to stand; and in the parliament itself Chaucer gives his most formal demonstration of how circumstance controls opinion. There is a single, clearly defined subject of discussion, in the problem of the love-rivalry of the three tercel eagles; and the opinions of the birds who speak are determined – it is comically obvious – by the nature of the species to which they belong, rather than by the nature of the problem. So the final decision is left to Nature herself:

> 'Now pes,' quod Nature, 'I comaunde heer!
> For I have herd al youre opynyoun,
> And in effect yit be we nevere the neer' . . .   (617–19)

The 'rout' of Canterbury pilgrims is the last and greatest of Chaucer's crowds. It is less multitudinous than Rumour's household or Nature's parliament (it would hardly count as a 'press') but large enough to contain an equal variety of members. These 'sondry folk, by aventure yfalle in felaweshipe' display to the full, in their tales and in their reactions to others' tales, those varieties of degree, age and 'complexion' which Chaucer describes in his Prologue. The

Knight's middle-aged tale of chivalry pleases everyone, young and old; but it pleases especially the 'gentils', and so provokes the Miller to redress the balance by telling a 'cherles tale in his manere'. This story has a mixed reception:

> Diverse folk diversely they seyde,
> But for the moore part they loughe and pleyde . . .
>
> (i. 3857–8)

And so on . . . The comparison with the *Parliament of Fowls*, which has occurred to several critics,[41] illuminates both this diversity of opinion and, especially, the figure who presides over it: the Host. Nature, who exercises the 'governaunce' in the *Parliament*, represents by her very definition the harmonious variety of the created universe; and she is therefore well qualified to preside, as she does with a measured and humorous tolerance, over the disputes into which the very natures of the different birds necessarily draw them. But as the 'vicaire of the almyghty Lord' Nature wields great authority; and when she dismisses the opinions of all the speakers in her final summing-up, the reader is offered a verdict against which there is no appeal. The Host, by contrast, derives his authority as 'governour' of the pilgrims solely from their grant of it as part of the scheme for making mirth which he proposed; and his final verdict on the best tale-teller would very likely, if we had it, provoke more doubts than it settled. The scheme of the *Canterbury Tales*, then, has no man of great authority raised above the level of the pilgrims. God's only 'vicaire' here is the Poor Parson, and he is a pilgrim, however admirable, like the rest of them. Yet the Host is an important figure nonetheless, exhibiting several curious similarities to Nature. Thanks to his occupation, he is socially amphibious; and his adaptability of speech, ranging from formal courtesy to downright bluntness, resembles Nature's. As a married man in the prime of life, he shares Nature's concern with 'engendrure'. But above all he is 'right a myrie man'; and his merriness, which reminds one rather of Bertilak than of Nature, is at the centre of the *Canterbury Tales*. The broad, strong, impartial humour which pervades so much Ricardian poetry pervades the *Canterbury Tales*; and its chief exponent is Harry Bailey. Blake was right to protest against those who think him no more than a figure of fun: 'The Host . . . is a first-rate character, and his jokes are no trifles; they are always, though uttered with audacity, and equally free with the Lord and

the Peasant, they are always substantially and weightily expressive
of knowledge and experience.'[42]

IV

Matthew Arnold said that Chaucer's 'view of things', his 'criticism
of life', had 'largeness, freedom, shrewdness, benignity', but lacked
'the high and excellent seriousness, which Aristotle assigns as one
of the grand virtues of poetry'. In an earlier chapter I admitted a
lack of 'high seriousness' in the style and manner of Ricardian
poets. They do not commonly speak directly to great matters. They
do not command the grand manner. Their characteristic tone of
voice lies in the, often equivocal, range between 'earnest' and 'game'.
It is now time further to admit that these stylistic limitations reflect, as they could hardly fail to do, limitations in these poets' view
of things. Arnold has been much abused for his judgment on
Chaucer; but it does apply, not only to Chaucer but also to Gower,
the *Gawain* poet, and even, in a way, to Langland.

The term 'middle-aged', which I used of the *Knight's Tale*
earlier, might be applied, more provocatively, to all Ricardian poetry.
Let us consider the term first in its negative significance. The Knight
(like his Theseus, I suggested) is of an age when he no longer shares
the preoccupations of Palamon or Arcite (or the Squire) and does
not yet share the other preoccupations of the aged Egeus. From
his middle position among the three ages of man, the Knight can
appreciate both the passionate Venerian vision of the young men
and also the old man's Saturnine vision of earth as nothing but
a 'thurghfare ful of wo'. But neither of these intensely serious
visions is the poem's vision. The Knight, like Theseus, sees courtly
love from the outside, humorously and even, on one occasion,
medically; and Arcite's death is treated with similar detachment,
not as an engrossing tragic event. The Knight gives medical
details again; and at the moment of death itself, his tone is so
guarded and unreverberant that Chaucer has been accused of
flippancy:[43]

> His spirit chaunged hous and wente ther,
> As I cam nevere, I kan nat tellen wher,
> Therfore I stynte, I nam no divinistre;
> Of soules fynde I nat in this registre,

Ne me ne list thilke opinions to telle
Of hem, though that they writen wher they dwelle . . .
(i. 2809-14)

The Knight is, of course, a fictional person; but I believe that nowhere else in his work does Chaucer decisively transcend the limitations of the Knight's vision; nor, perhaps, do his contemporaries.

In the persons of Troilus and Amans, Chaucer and Gower give portraits of lovers unparalleled for vividness and detail in previous English poetry. But these are portraits *ab extra*: the poet does not write 'with ful devout corage', nor does he write 'de sentement'. Chaucer tells us that he has never experienced love himself, and Gower that his love is spent. These may be fictions, but they are fictions which match and support a particular treatment of love – sympathetic and understanding, but distant. Hence the omnipresent humour and irony; hence, too, that annoying 'twinkle'. For the irony is not always pleasing or appropriate. There are times, as when Pandarus brings a cushion for Troilus to kneel on beside Criseyde's bed, when the jokes seem to spring, not from wisdom or subtlety on the author's part, but from incapacity, a real failure of 'seriousness'. It is not so much that Chaucer succeeds in stepping outside the passionate world of Troilus as that he fails to stay inside it. His humour, here, seems to form part of a strategy of self-defence against the full intensity of youthful experience in 'love-service' – the intensity which Dante, chief among several medieval poets outside England, so thoroughly accepts and so unreservedly expresses.

Irony and humour sometimes play a similar defensive role in relation to the kind of seriousness which Egeus and Saturn represent – what Dante calls the 'gravity and severity' of old age confronted with human frailty, solitude and death.[44] Gawain's solitary approach to what he supposes is certain death at the Green Chapel is richly orchestrated by the poet and embellished, as it were, with fragments of *Dies Irae*; but the terrible vision of last things dissolves into sociable laughter and a fairy-tale ending. Gower's poem leaves Amans with his first intimations of an old age whose true character is only dimly suggested by the black beads inscribed *Por reposer* which Venus gives him. The poem, after hovering on the brink of love for so long, ends on the brink of the other solitude and intensity of old age, but still with a smile and a touch of complacency.

One is reminded of the epigraph to T. S. Eliot's *Gerontion*:

> Thou hast nor youth nor age
> But as it were an after dinner sleep
> Dreaming of both.

In the richer, more comprehensive work of Chaucer, the vision of earth as a thoroughfare full of woe is much more generously represented; but the *contemptus mundi* is, with one possible exception, never wholly endorsed and hence never expressed in its full grandeur. It remains a point of view, albeit a most authoritative one. The *Parliament of Fowls* is not committed to the opinions of Cicero ('oure present worldes lyves space / Nis but a maner deth') so cautiously expressed as a summary of a book the dreamer happened to read in search of another kind of knowledge, any more than the *Knight's Tale* is committed to the kindred opinions of Egeus. Nor does the *Parson's Tale*, even in the commanding position which it occupies at the end of our *Canterbury Tales,* cease to be the *Parson's Tale.* Not that it is an object of purely aesthetic and documentary interest, like the Jesuit sermon in *Portrait of the Artist as a Young Man*: it has truth in it. But this is not the whole truth of the *Canterbury Tales.*[45] Even the closing stanzas of *Troilus,* which most readers would count, together with some passages from *Piers,* as representing the rare achievement of a true religious sublimity in Ricardian poetry, are taken by some good critics with a grain of salt.[46] Even if these critics are wrong, their readings provide remarkable evidence of the way Chaucer disposes his reader to respond cautiously to anything resembling a 'flight', and to be always on his guard for the ironic implication, the humorous cross-light.

The effect of these limitations in Ricardian poetry may be indicated by describing the special hungers which a persistent reader of this poetry develops, as if from deficiencies of diet. He hungers for grandeur of thought, unguarded intensity of feeling, and sublimity of expression. He wants 'earnest', for once, *without* 'game'. He feels how much Chaucer misses, in the *House of Fame* and elsewhere, out of Virgil, and how little of the majesty of Arthurian legend survives in *Sir Gawain.* So he turns elsewhere, to Virgil or Dante or Wordsworth, to find great subjects – love, death, war – treated greatly, without humour of irony; and he learns to appreciate 'seriousness' even in the poetry of Matthew Arnold himself.

But from these poets, in turn, he may learn to appreciate better what is so powerfully there in Ricardian poetry, backing up the mundane humour and unheroic ironies. 'Middle-aged' is, after all, too dim and negative a term to apply to those vigorous and eminently characteristic figures, no longer young but not yet old, who occupy such an important place in the poetry of this period and set its tone. These are men in the prime of active life, jovial men, both in the astrological sense and in the modern sense which derives from it, and they bestride the poems in which they appear. Harry Bailey, Theseus and Pandarus all belong to this group, as does Sir Bertilak, whom the poet introduces in the following very typical passage:

> A hoge hathel for the nonez, and of hyghe eldee;
> Brode, bryght, watz his berde, and al bever-hwed,
> Sturne, stif on the stryththe on stalworth schonkez,
> Felle face as the fyre, and fre of hys speche;
> And wel hym semed, for sothe, as the segge thught,
> To lede a lortschyp in lee of leudez ful gode . . .   (844–9)

Like Theseus, Pandarus and the Host, Bertilak is 'of hyghe eldee', at the top of that arc to which Dante in the *Convivio* compares the course of human life; and we see him in the mature roles of householder and host. He is also a married man, like Theseus and Harry Bailey, as well as Piers (and Will) in *Piers Plowman*. In all these poems – the *Knight's Tale*, the *Canterbury Tales, Troilus, Sir Gawain* and *Piers* – the 'governaunce' belongs to a character who has his roots in quotidian and even domestic realities. In *Confessio Amantis*, we miss such a figure; and its absence there seems to be associated with a certain weakness which most readers – certainly most readers of Chaucer – feel in the poem.

These figures, with their characteristic 'jovial' wisdom, embody an image of man which is not heroic, not romantic, and not at all 'monkish'. It is an image of 'high eld' which stands at the centre of Ricardian poetry, an ideal of 'mesure' which involves that sober acceptance of things as they are which Theseus advocates:

> Thanne is it wysdom, as it thynketh me,
> To maken vertu of necessitee,
> And take it weel that we may nat eschue.
>
> (*C.T.* i. 3041–2)

Here is the 'largeness, freedom, shrewdness, benignity' which Arnold allowed Chaucer; but also what he denied him, a kind of 'high seriousness'.

Chapter Four

Conclusion

I

Every age looks both back to the past and forward to the future, and every generation of poets faces both ways. The generation of Chaucer and the *Gawain* poet looks back as far as Anglo-Saxon times and forward as far as the nineteenth, if not the twentieth, century. What is more exceptional, the range of its backward-and-forward view takes in such radically different types of poetic activity as those of the Anglo-Saxon scop and medieval minstrel on the one side and the modern literary artist on the other. Because of this unusual 'range', the contrasts between old and new in Ricardian poetry are exceptionally bold and challenging. The poet's performance will at times be old-fashioned, even archaic, in its observance of traditional, non-personal norms; at other times it will be unmistakably original, modern and individual. Such antinomies make themselves felt in every aspect of Ricardian writings, whether style, or characterization, or plotting, or thematic development; and they demand from the reader no little tact and agility in response. The ideal reader of Ricardian poetry should be trained in the school of Renaissance and post-Renaissance writing to appreciate the subtleties of individual literary artistry; but in addition he should possess the ability, not merely to recognize where such artistry is not in question, but also to appreciate fully those other kinds of composition which acquiesce in *common* stories and themes and expressions. Since the history of taste suggests that these two kinds of appreciation tend to flourish at each other's expense, it would seem difficult for anyone to achieve an entirely just and balanced view of the relations between tradition and the individual talent in the Ricardian period. But especially where problems of 'originality' are concerned, a modern reader can hardly avoid the challenge to balance his responses at least roughly.

To illustrate what is demanded of him, it will be worth while to select a single, fairly typical feature of Ricardian poetry for discussion. Let us therefore consider the different kinds of *simile* which these poets use.

Some of the similes in Ricardian poetry exhibit the familiar characteristics of the literary simile as practised in the English 'art tradition'. In this kind of simile, the points of comparison between the two things compared ('tenor' and 'vehicle') tend to be chosen by the author with an eye to the unexpected or subtle connection. Also the simile may express some otherwise fugitive characteristic of the tenor; and the vehicle will be evoked with some degree of independent, often richly musical and poetic, description. Of the four poets under discussion here, Chaucer is the most given to this kind of simile; and examples are easiest to find, as we might expect, in his *Troilus*.[1] The most striking is the battery of three similes with which he introduces Troilus' first night of love with Criseyde. The passage is worth quoting at length:

> Criseyde, al quyt from every drede and tene,
> As she that juste cause hadde hym to triste,
> Made hym swich feste, it joye was to seene,
> Whan she his trouthe and clene entente wiste;
> And as aboute a tree, with many a twiste,
> Bytrent and writh the swote wodebynde,
> Gan ech of hem in armes other wynde.
>
> And as the newe abaysed nyghtyngale,
> That stynteth first whan she bygynneth to synge,
> Whan that she hereth any herde tale,
> Or in the hegges any wyght stirynge,
> And after siker doth hire vois out rynge,
> Right so Criseyde, whan hire drede stente,
> Opned hire herte, and tolde hym hire entente.
>
> And right as he that seth his deth yshapen,
> And dyen not, in ought that he may gesse,
> And sodeynly rescous doth hym escapen,
> And from his deth is brought in sykernesse,
> For al this world, in swych present gladnesse
> Was Troilus, and hath his lady swete . . .   (iii. 1226–45)

In this very carefully planned sequence, the simple and sensuous simile of the woodbine, referring to the mutual embraces of Troilus and Criseyde, is followed by two more elaborate comparisons, referring one to Criseyde, the other to Troilus. Criseyde's is a delicate pastoral miniature of hedges and shepherds, and describes her recovery of confidence after the interval of 'drede and tene' caused by Pandarus' story of Troilus' jealousy. The comparison is quite complex, since it involves not only Criseyde's recovery from the check administered by Pandarus (who corresponds to the talkative shepherd), but also the fact that before the check she was beginning to conquer her fears and yield to her confidence in Troilus: 'that stynteth first *whan she bygynneth to synge*'. Troilus' simile also concerns present security, and the 'sykernesse' of 1243 recalls the 'siker' of 1237. But its content is grimmer, as befits the case of one whose life really is at stake.[2] In exploring such subtleties the modern reader can feel quite at home. These similes are in the post-medieval manner. They have their descendants even in the poetry of T. S. Eliot:

> I said to my soul, be still, and let the dark come upon you
> Which shall be the darkness of God. As, in a theatre,
> The lights are extinguished, for the scene to be changed
> With a hollow rumble of wings, with a movement of darkness
> on darkness,
> And we know that the hills and the trees, the distant panorama
> And the bold imposing façade are all being rolled away –
> Or as, when an underground train, in the tube, stops too long
> between stations
> And the conversation rises and slowly fades into silence
> And you see behind every face the mental emptiness deepen
> Leaving only the growing terror of nothing to think about;
> Or when, under ether, the mind is conscious but conscious of
> nothing –
> I said to my soul, be still, and wait without hope . . .
>
> (*East Coker*)

These comparisons are more far-fetched than Chaucer's; but the sustained phrasing and the choice of felicitous detail (such as 'a hollow rumble of *wings*') place Eliot in the same tradition.

None of Chaucer's contemporaries attempts anything quite like the similes in *Troilus*. The nearest Gower gets is in similes of that heroic kind which later appealed to Lydgate, where warriors are compared to some fierce animal, thus:

> Lich to the chaced wylde bor,
> The houndes whan he fieleth sor,
> Tothroweth and goth forth his weie,
> In such a wise forto seie
> This worthi kniht with swerd on honde
> His weie made . . .   (vii. 5255–60)

But Chaucer does this kind of thing better, especially in the *Knight's Tale* (e.g. i. 1637–48). In general Gower's similes are less elaborate and beautiful, more inclined to be baldly instructive, than Chaucer's.[3] Langland also tends in his longer similes towards a more instructive type which, in the words of one critic, 'bears some resemblance both to the traditional "Homeric" simile and to the exemplum'.[4] But Langland's *exempla* often achieve great poetic beauty, as in this passage from the A-text (which is, however, omitted from B and C):

> Right as a rose, that red is and swet,
> Out of a raggit rote and a rough brere
> Springeth and spredith, that spiceris desirith,
> Or as whete out of weed waxith, out of the erthe,
> So dobest out of dobet and dowel gynneth springe
> Among men of this molde that mek ben and kynde . . .
> (A x. 123–8)[5]

The *Gawain* poet does not often employ the elaborated 'Homeric' simile; but he also is capable of doing so to great effect. There is a compact example in *Sir Gawain*, in a passage describing how the hero stands to receive the return blow:

> Gawayn graythely hit bydez, and glent with no membre,
> Bot stode stylle as the ston, other a stubbe auther
> That ratheled is in roché grounde with rotez a hundreth . . .
> (2292–4)

Here a simple proverbial comparison, of the kind we shall discuss shortly, is coupled with a more elaborate and artistic simile. The coupling is supported by the customary pairing of 'stock' (stub) with 'stone'; but, for most modern readers at least, the second simile quite overshadows the first, because the alliterative linking of 'ratheled', 'roché' and 'rotez' in the adjectival clause makes its significance explicit in a vivid way. The poet's finest similes of this sort are to be found in *Pearl*, however. Describing the precious stones at the bottom of the paradisal stream, he writes there:

> In the founce ther stonden stones stepe,
> As glente thurgh glas that glowed and glyght,
> As stremande sternes, quen strothe-men slepe,
> Staren in welkyn in wynter nyght . . .   (113–16)

This double simile expresses not only the brightness of the jewels but also the clearness of the element through which they shine; and the addition of the adverbial clause 'quen strothe-men slepe' converts the second comparison into a miniature idyll, like Chaucer's simile of the nightingale. More delicate still is the simile the poet uses to convey the marvellous, sudden appearance of the procession in the Heavenly Jerusalem:

> Ryght as the maynful mone con rys
> Er thenne the day-glem dryve al doun,
> So sodanly on a wonder wyse
> I watz war of a prosessyoun . . .   (1093–6)

Like T. S. Eliot in the passage quoted earlier from the *Four Quartets*, the poet here compares not things but experiences: the experience of seeing the procession 'sodanly on a wonder wyse' is compared to the experience of catching sight of the moon in the evening sky before the sun has set. The abstract, almost metaphysical quality of this comparison reminds one of Dante, the greatest master of literary simile.[6]

The similes so far discussed all belong to the tradition most familiar to a modern reader of conventional tastes. But the *Gawain* poet and his contemporaries also use similes of less familiar kinds. Perhaps their most characteristic type is represented by the *Gawain* poet's description in *Patience* of how Jonah went into the mouth of the whale:

> As mote in at a munster dor, so mukel wern his chawles . . .
> (268)

This is the drastic kind of simile. Here the effect is graphic, often grotesque, and sometimes humorous. *Purity* has a number of remarkable examples. The fall of the angels from heaven is described as follows:

Fellen fro the fyrmament fendez ful blake,
Sweved at the fyrst swap as the snaw thikke,
Hurled into helle-hole as the hyve swarmez.
Fylter fenden folk forty dayez lencthe,
Er that styngande storme stynt ne myght;
Bot as smylt mele under smal sive smokez forthikke,
So fro heven to helle that hatel schor laste . . .   (221–7)

Here, as in the example from *Gawain* noticed previously, the poet starts with a proverbial comparison: 'Thick as snow'.[7] There follows the image of swarming bees, which anticipates Milton (*Paradise Lost* i. 768–75). This is vivid, and seems to be original; but it is overshadowed by the extraordinary simile which completes the sequence: the shower of falling angels compared to meal smoking under a fine sieve. Later in the same poem, in an equally drastic comparison, the destruction of the country of Sodom and Gomorrah is compared to the disintegration of a badly-bound manuscript book:

And cloven alle in lyttel cloutes the clyffez aywhere,
As lance levez of the boke that lepes in twynne . . . (965–6)

The sheer unexpectedness, the total absence of any previous association between tenor and vehicle, indeed the incongruity between them, is what marks this kind of simile off from the more traditional 'poetic' type.

Some of the best-known examples of drastic simile occur in Langland's grotesque descriptions of the Seven Deadly Sins. Envy looks 'as a leke hadde yleye longe in the sonne' (v. 82); the cheeks of Avarice hang down 'as a letheren purs' (v. 192); and after a day's drinking Gluttony,

thanne gan he go liche a glewmannes bicche,
Somme tyme aside and somme tyme arrere,
As who-so leyth lynes forto lacche foules . . .   (v. 353–5)

The minstrel's bitch is presumably a dog trained to walk on its hind legs as part of the varied entertainment which minstrels provided.[8] The coupling of this image with that of a man moving irregularly about as he lays a bird-trap illustrates how boldly Langland handles his similes. The two disparate images, superimposed upon the image of the staggering drunkard, create an appropriately phantasmagoric effect. Later in the poem, in another passage concerning

K   135

the Deadly Sins, there is a simpler example of this same boldness. Hawkin is guilty of wrath and envy, and he seeks vengeance on his enemies:

> Avenge me fele tymes, other frete myselve
> Wythinne, as a shepster shere . . .   (xiii. 330–1)

'On many occasions I take vengeance, or else fret myself inwardly like a pair of sheep-shears.' The comparison of Hawkin's frustrated rancour to the grating and wearing of shear blades on their inside surface is far-fetched; but like most of Langland's comparisons, it carries conviction.

Even the sober and correct Gower indulges in this kind of simile, most remarkably in a passage describing a slothful man having nightmares:

> Bot thanne who so toke kepe,
> Whanne he is falle in such a drem,
> Riht as a schip ayein the strem,
> He routeth with a slepi noise,
> And brustleth as a monkes froise
> Whanne it is throwe into the panne . . . (iv. 2728–33)

The images of a ship moving against the current and a monk's pan-cake sizzling in a frying-pan are as heterogeneous as anything in *Piers Plowman*; but they seem more grotesque than apt. Here, as in the comparison of the griffin's egg noted in a previous chapter, Gower's use of drastic simile seems something of a mannerism. Perhaps it should be understood as a concession to a contemporary stylistic fashion. But Gower does sometimes achieve a humorous effect, as when the Loathly Lady offers herself to the reluctant Florent 'lich unto the wollesak' (i. 1692).

Chaucer exercises restraint in the use of drastic simile. He hardly uses it at all in *Troilus*;[9] and even in the *House of Fame*, where the fantastic descriptions of the houses of Fame and Rumour might seem to invite extravagance, he stops short (though sometimes only just short) of the most drastic type. Typical examples from the latter poem are the following:

> The halle was al ful, ywys,
> Of hem that writen olde gestes,
> As ben on trees rokes nestes . . .   (1514–16)[10]

> thrughout every regioun
> Wente this foule trumpes soun,
> As swifte as pelet out of gonne,
> Whan fyr is in the poudre ronne.
> And such a smoke gan out wende
> Out of his foule trumpes ende,
> Blak, bloo, grenyssh, swartish red,
> As doth where that men melte led ...   (1641–8)

In the *Canterbury Tales,* too, Chaucer is bold without extravagance. The comparison of January's bristly cheeks to 'the skyn of hound-fyssh' in the *Merchant's Tale* (iv. 1825) is less far-fetched than it seems, since medieval carpenters used dog-fish skin for sandpaper.[11] There are, however, many moderately drastic similes in the *Canter-bury Tales.* In the General Prologue, the Monk's eyes gleam 'as a forneys of a leed', the hair on the Miller's wart is 'reed as the brustles of a sowes erys', and his mouth 'as greet was as a greet forneys'. From the tales themselves one example must be sufficient:

> And as a bitore bombleth in the myre,
> She leyde hir mouth unto the water doun:
> 'Biwreye me nat, thou water, with thy soun' ...
>
>   (iii. 972–4)

All the similes so far discussed are, at least to some degree, original. They all represent either new aspects of a relationship already perceived by others (Gower's simile of the boar, the *Gawain* poet's simile of the tree-trunk) or a relationship perceived for the first time (Chaucer's simile of the bittern, Langland's of the performing dog and the bird-trapper). In all these cases the reader of modern poetry can rely upon his customary responses, even if some of the more drastic similes may not be to his taste. But the majority of the similes in Ricardian verse are of a different sort altogether, and demand a different response. These are what we may call 'proverbial' similes. They are found in profusion in the work of all the Ricardian poets except Gower, who uses them relatively little;[12] and they present, in their old-fashioned simplicity, something of a stumbling-block for a sophisticated modern reader accustomed to look for novelty or subtlety or individuality in poetic figures.

Not all similes classable as 'proverbial' present such difficulties.

Sometimes the Ricardian poet amplifies the comparison, usually with an adjectival phrase or clause, and to that extent makes it his own. Examples of such 'touched up' comparisons are:

> As chaste as a childe *that in cherche wepeth*   (*Piers* i. 178)
> Schyrer then snawe *that schedez on hillez*   (*Gawain* 956)
> As fressh as faukoun *comen out of muwe*   (*Troilus* iii. 1784)
> As glysnande golde *that man con schere* (*Pearl* 165).[13]

Sometimes, again, the simple comparison is used unamplified but in a context which invests it with some singular significance, often ironic or humorous. The misapplication of the simile 'ruddy as a rose' to the gluttonous friar in *Piers Plowman* (discussed above, p. 34) illustrates a technique which Chaucer also uses, most obviously in *Sir Thopas*:

> Sire Thopas wax a doghty swayn;
> Whit was his face as payndemayn,
> His lippes rede as rose . . .   (vii. 724–6)

In the General Prologue, another poetic-proverbial simile is applied unexpectedly, in this case to the Friar:

> His nekke whit was as the flour-de-lys . . .   (i. 238)

Chaucer shows special mastery in discovering all kinds of new uses for old similes. One example must stand for many. In the *Squire's Tale*, Canacee comes upon a falcon in a tree:

> Amydde a tree, for drye as whit as chalk,
> As Canacee was pleyyng in hir walk,
> Ther sat a faucon over hire heedful hye . . . (v. 409–11)

The simile 'white as chalk' was proverbial, even commonplace (one might compare the epithet 'chalk-white' in *Gawain* 798); but in its application to the strange dry, white tree it gains extra meaning, because chalk is dry as well as white, and makes a powerful contribution to the extraordinary atmosphere of this whole episode in the Squire's story.

But it cannot be said that Ricardian poets usually amplify or 'misapply' the similes which they draw from common stock; nor is the kind of originality which I illustrated from the *Squire's Tale* as common as one might wish it to be. In a very large number of cases, the proverbial simile seems to mean no more (and no less) in the poet's context than it would in any other. In the description of Sir Gawain standing firm to receive the Green Knight's blow (quoted above, p. 133), the proverbial 'still as the stone' does perhaps receive some increment of meaning from the very fact that the immediately succeeding image of the 'stubbe' outdoes it: a rock is less easily moved than a man, but more easily than a rooted tree. But in the three places where Gower uses the same simile, the meaning is quite unmodified by his contexts;[14] and Chaucer also tends to use it straight. Of the eleven occurrences in his work, most are like this one from *Troilus*:

> Criseyde aros, no lenger she ne stente,
> But streght into hire closet wente anon,
> And set hire doun as stylle as any ston . . .
>
> (ii. 598–600)[15]

Perhaps the most pregnant of the five uses in *Troilus* is the last, where the simile expresses (with the help of verbal play on 'ston . . . astoned') the final dumbfounding of the loquacious Pandarus:

> For sory of his frendes sorwe he is,
> And shamed for his nece hath don amys,
> And stant, astoned of thise causes tweye,
> As stille as ston; a word ne kowde he seye . . .
>
> (v. 1726–9)

But even here the effect is very simple, certainly by comparison with the elaborately literary similes which we meet elsewhere in the same poem.

The publication of B. J. Whiting's great collection of material makes it easy to confirm one's impression that the Ricardian poets are, with the partial exception of Gower, as free with proverbial comparisons as any of their Middle English predecessors. Their work abounds in phrases such as hot as fire, true as steel, cold as a key, dead as a doornail, naked as a needle, white as bone, black as coal, brown as a berry, red as a rose. Examples of these and many other similar phrases have been collected by Whiting, as well as examples of a slightly more elaborate type such as 'glad as fowl of day' or 'white as blossom on bough'.[16] Such similes contribute greatly to the equivocal 'intensive' style of description – sometimes ironical, sometimes naïve, and often doubtful – which we noted in a previous chapter. They also present a striking contrast to the literary similes, both traditional and 'drastic', with which they are freely mingled. The very meticulous and personal art which produced the elaborate similes of *Troilus* also drew heavily on common stock, on the *communis sententia* of a broad medieval vernacular. The reader of this poetry, therefore, needs to be able both to care and not to care about things like artistic originality and freshness of perception. Such qualities are present in Ricardian writing, and no amount of argument about the conventionality of medieval poetry will conceal the fact; but there is also a readiness to accept common forms of speech even where these seem to usurp the poet's peculiar privileges in metaphor, simile and the other tropes. Proverbial comparisons do play a considerable part in the style of later English art poetry, especially in the early modern period. But Ricardian poetry exhibits a balance, an equipollence of the two types of simile, literary and proverbial, which seems peculiar to it. In earlier Middle English poetry, the main type is proverbial; in modern English, the literary type becomes increasingly dominant. In the poetry of Chaucer and his contemporaries both types demand almost equal attention, though attention of a different kind. One last quotation from the *Gawain* poet will illustrate this balance:

> For uch mon had mervayle quat hit mene myght
> That a hathel and a horse myght such a hwe lach,
> As growe grene as the gres and grener hit semed,
> Then grene aumayl on golde glowande bryghter . . .
>
> (233–6)

This is another of the poet's favourite double similes. The first comparison, 'grene as the gres', obviously comes out of common stock. The second, equally obviously, is created for the occasion. Green enamel glowing against a gold background provides a novel standard of vividness. It recalls other combinations of green and gold in the equipment of the Green Knight: the silk trappings embroidered with 'gay gaudi of grene, the golde ay inmyddes', the green hairs of the horse's tail twined with gold thread 'ay a herle of the here, an other of golde', and the blade of the axe 'al of grene stele and of golde hewen'. In tracing subtleties of this kind the modern reader feels at home. For him the greater difficulty will be to respond adequately to the simple, common-stock comparison with grass, as the poem also requires us to do.

The *Gawain* poet's double simile illustrates in little that particular mixture of conservatism and innovation which we have encountered in Ricardian poetry throughout this study, and also the flexibility of response which this mixture requires of the reader.

II

In the passage which I quoted earlier, Wimsatt and Beardsley refer to 'the great English art tradition (Chaucer to Tennyson)'. In naming Tennyson as the terminus of this tradition they had questions of metre in mind; but it is not only in metre that twentieth-century poetry in English has begun to move away from the English art tradition. The complex changes in literary taste associated with this movement have already affected and no doubt will continue to affect our view of the Ricardian poetry. Earlier critics' commitment to the Chaucer of the art tradition is beginning to appear a little dated and parochial. Chaucer now seems a less Tennysonian poet, metrically and otherwise, than he used to. His contemporaries are enjoying more attention in their own right, some of it from readers who no longer value the meticulous verbal artistry of the 'great' English tradition. Our attitude towards popular and common-stock elements in poetry ('green as the grass') is changing.

Perhaps, as I suggested in the Introduction, such developments will contribute in the future to a more synoptic view of the Ricardian period than has been possible up to now. One cannot anticipate these developments. Borges writes: 'If I were granted the possibility of reading any present-day page as it will be read in the year two thousand, I would know what the literature of the year two thousand will be like.' To read a page of *Troilus* or *Piers* as it will be read in the year 2000 would equally require knowledge of what the literature of that year will be like. The present book can hardly claim to represent 1971, let alone 2000. Critics who stand more outside the English 'art tradition' than I do will no doubt be able to frame hypotheses which will represent more truly and explain more powerfully the various characteristics exhibited by poets of the Ricardian period. But I hope to have established at least that it *is*, in something like the full literary sense, a period.

Notes and References

Introduction

1   Chaucer's career as a writer, from the *Book of the Duchess* (not earlier than 1369, usually dated about 1370) until his death in 1400, coincides with this period. The first, A, version of *Piers Plowman* was dated 1362 by Skeat; but Huppé (*PMLA*, liv [1939], 37–64) and Bennett (*PMLA*, lviii [1943], 566–72) argue for a date in the next decade, and 1370 seems a likely year on the evidence presented by Bennett. Langland worked on the B-version between 1377 and 1379. C is now usually dated before 1387. Gower's *Confessio Amantis* was first published in 1390, and the latest revised edition is not later than 1393. Gower lived until 1408; but his last work *In Praise of Peace* belongs, like Chaucer's *Complaint to his Purse,* to the first months of Henry IV's reign. Cotton Nero A.x. is generally dated about 1400, but there is no clear evidence for the dates of its contents: *Sir Gawain* is placed tentatively by its latest editor 'towards the end of the century', and Gordon suggests that *Pearl* belongs 'late rather than early' in a period *c.* 1360–95.

2   Peyre, H., *Les Générations littéraires*, Paris, 1948, 13. Peyre's own method of distinguishing 'literary generations' by the dates of authors' births cannot be used in the present case, since the dates are all uncertain. It would be rash to call our poets 'the generation of 1340'.

3   Rickert, E., 'King Richard II's Books' in *Library*, 4th Series, xiii (1933), 144–7. See also Loomis, R. S., in *Studies in Language, Literature and Culture of the Middle Ages and After*, ed. Atwood, E. B., and Hill, A. A., Texas, 1969, 173–8.

4   *Confessio* Prologue 34*f (first recension). In the F-Prologue to the *Legend of Good Women* Chaucer expresses the intention of presenting the poem to Queene Anne (496–7). See generally Mathew, G., *The Court of Richard II,* London, 1968, and Harvey, J., *Gothic England*, 2nd ed., London, 1948.

5   See René Wellek on the theory of literary periodization, 'Periods and Movements in Literary History' in *English Institute Annual 1940*, New York, 1941, 73–93; whence Wellek and Warren, *Theory of Literature,* London, 1949, 274 ff.

6   Wimsatt, W. K., and Beardsley, M. K., 'The Concept of Metre' in Wimsatt, *Hateful Contraries*, Lexington, Kentucky, 1965, 127.

7   On the relationship between Chaucer and Gower, see the very elaborate

study by Fisher, J. H., *John Gower: Moral Philosopher and Friend of Chaucer,* London, 1965, especially Chapter 5.

8   On the relationship between Chaucer and Langland, see Coghill, N., 'Two Notes on *Piers Plowman*', *Medium Aevum,* iv (1935), 89–94; and most recently Bennett, J. A. W., 'Chaucer's Contemporary' in Hussey, S.S. (ed.), *Piers Plowman: Critical Approaches,* London, 1969, 310–24. The latter essay is very relevant to the argument of the present book. On Chaucer and *Gawain,* see Chapman, C. O., 'Chaucer and the *Gawain*-Poet: a Conjecture' in *Modern Language Notes,* lxviii (1953), 521–4.

9   Difficulties of interpreting Chaucer's Parson are illustrated in Blake, N. F., 'Chaucer and the Alliterative Romances' in *Chaucer Review,* iii (1969), 163–9. See also Everett, D., *Essays on Middle English Literature,* Oxford, 1955, Chapter VI.

10   Hulbert, J. R., 'A Hypothesis Concerning the Alliterative Revival' in *Modern Philology,* xxviii (1930–1), 405–22; discussed by Salter, E., 'The Alliterative Revival' in *Modern Philology,* lxiv (1966–7), 146–50, 233–7, who accepts the association between alliterative verse and the higher nobility of the West, but rejects the political motive.

11   Menner, R. J. (ed.), *Purity,* New Haven, 1920, xix–xxvii; Robbins, R. H., 'A *Gawain* Epigone' in *Modern Language Notes,* lviii (1943), 361–6. Also *PMLA,* lxv (1950), 249–81.

12   Warton, Thomas, *The History of English Poetry* [ed. Richard Price], 4 vols., London, 1824, i. 187–8.

13   The total of fifty-one does not include fragmentary MSS. See Donaldson, E. T., *Piers Plowman: The C-Text and Its Poet* (revised ed.), London, 1966, 3, and list of MSS. in Appendix A.

14   Skeat, W. W., *The Vision of William Concerning Piers the Plowman,* Part IV, E.E.T.S., 1877–84, 863. Allusions to *Piers* are collected, 863–74. See also Donaldson, op. cit., 3 ff.

15   Spenser, E., *Shepheardes Calender,* Epilogue, l. 10; Puttenham, *Arte of English Poesie,* in Gregory Smith, G. (ed.), *Elizabethan Critical Essays,* Oxford, 1904, ii. 27; Milton, J., *Apology against a Pamphlet,* in Columbia *Works,* New York, 1931, iii. 329.

16   Warton, Thomas, *The History of English Poetry,* i (1774), Section VIII.

17   For these references see Spurgeon, C. F. E., *Five Hundred Years of Chaucer Criticism and Allusion, 1357–1900,* Cambridge, 1925.

18   *Jo. Gower de Confessione Amantis* (1532). On the history of Gower's reputation see Fisher, J. H., op. cit., Chapter 1, 'Critical Reputation'; also Spies, H., 'Bisherige Ergebnisse und weitere Aufgaben der Gower-forschung' in *Englische Studien,* xxviii (1900), 163–74.

19   Ed. Gregory Smith, i. 152.

20   Ed. Gregory Smith, ii. 62.

21   Broadus, E. K., *The Laureateship,* Oxford, 1921, 61. On the development of this tradition see Broadus, 16–19; also Fisher, op. cit., 19.

22   Three Latin poems written for Henry IV by Gower late in 1399 are named 'the laureate group' by Fisher, op. cit., 99. See also Coffman, G. R., 'John Gower, Mentor for Royalty: Richard II' in *PMLA,* lxix (1954), 953–64.

23 *The History of English Poetry*, ii (1778), 1.

24 Lewis, C. S., *The Allegory of Love*, Oxford, 1936, 198–222.

25 From a poem composed at Stowey, recorded in the margin of a copy of *Sibylline Leaves*, printed by Lowes, J. L., *The Road to Xanadu*, 2nd ed., London, 1951, 471, note 145.

26 In MSS. which appear closest to Gower's usage (e.g. Fairfax 3), þ is found regularly, except in capital position and in some foreign words (Macaulay, Introduction, xcvii). In MSS. which appear closest to Chaucer's usage (e.g. the Ellesmere and Hengwrt Canterbury Tales, and the Peterhouse Equatorie, which may be in Chaucer's own hand), þ is used chiefly in the abbreviated form þᵗ (that), and occasionally elsewhere: see Price, D. J. (ed.), *The Equatorie of the Planetis*, Cambridge, 1955, 141.

27 In the present book, when quoting from Skeat's E.E.T.S. edition of *Piers*, Davis's *Sir Gawain*, Gordon's *Pearl*, Menner's *Purity* and Anderson's *Patience* (see Preface, p. vii), I have altered the spelling where necessary in order to bring the usage into line with that of Robinson's Chaucer and Macaulay's Gower. The distribution of u/v and i/j has been modernized; *th* has been substituted for þ; *y* or *gh* or *w* has been substituted for ȝ. (This letter, the yogh, does not appear in MSS. closest to Chaucer's usage; but Gower has it commonly for *y*, though not for *gh*: Macaulay, Introduction, xcvi–xcvii). These alterations sometimes produce unfortunate results (e.g. *yye* for *yȝe*); but uniformity in the presentation of the texts seems desirable in the present study. It would also seem desirable, on the same principles, that the next learned edition of Chaucer should follow the usage of the MSS. more closely.

28 Wellek, R., art. cit., 91.

29 A standard treatment may be found in Baugh, A. C. (ed.), *A Literary History of England*, 2nd ed., London, 1967. The volume of the Oxford History devoted to this period has not yet appeared.

30 On Thomas Chestre, see most recently Mills, M. (ed.), *Lybeaus Desconus*, E.E.T.S., 1969, 64–8. Clanvowe's *Boke of Cupide* is edited by Scattergood, V. J., *English Philological Studies*, ix (1965), 47–83. The exclusion of such writers may well seem arbitrary; but I agree with Wellek that the idea of a period as a 'time section dominated by a whole system of norms' is not to be conceived of statistically: 'It is entirely possible to envisage a situation in which older norms still prevailed numerically while the new conventions were created or used by writers of greatest artistic importance. It thus seems to me impossible to avoid the critical problem of evaluation in literary history.' *Concepts of Criticism*, New Haven, 1963, 129.

Chapter 1

1 See especially Curtius, E. R., *European Literature and the Latin Middle Ages*, trans. Trask, W. R., London, 1953, and Faral, E., *Les arts poétiques du XIIe et du XIIIe siècle*, Paris, 1958.

2 See for example Cottle, B., *The Triumph of English 1350–1400*, London, 1969; also Suggett, H., 'The Use of French in England in the Later Middle Ages' in Southern, R. W. (ed.), *Essays in Medieval History*, London, 1968.

3 Individual poets of an earlier period had in some degree anticipated Ricardian developments, of course. An example is the author of *Kyng Alisaunder* (London, late thirteenth-century). Since this poem appeared in the Auchinleck MS. (now mutilated at the place), it may have been known to Chaucer: see below, note 12.

4 The phrase is used by Mehl, D., *Middle English Romances of the Thirteenth and Fourteenth Centuries*, London, 1969, 13; see generally 7–13, with valuable references.

5 The term is so used by Olson, C. C., 'The Minstrels at the Court of Edward III' in *PMLA*, lvi (1941), 601–12. Cf. Gower, *Confessio Amantis* vii. 2423–4: 'every menstral hadde pleid, / And every disour hadde seid'.

6 See Baugh, A. C., 'The Authorship of the Middle English Romances' in *Annual Bulletin of the Modern Humanities Research Association*, xxii (1950), 13–28, and 'The Middle English Romance: Some Questions of Creation, Presentation, and Preservation' in *Speculum*, xlii (1967), 1–31. In the latter Baugh concludes: 'Minstrel authorship of the Middle English romances was the exception, not the rule' (p. 5).

7 The author of *Reinbrun* (in the Auchinleck MS.) includes 'romaunce reding' among the accomplishments of the African princess (12.10–12).

8 See *M.E.D.* under *disour* and *gestour*. Chaucer's term was *gestour*: *House of Fame* 1198, *Canterbury Tales* vii. 846.

9 The term *clérigo ajuglarado* is applied to Juan Ruiz by Menéndez Pidal, R., in *Poesía juglaresca y juglares*, Madrid, 1924, 265.

10 Baugh, A. C., *Speculum*, xlii (1967), 9–10, observes that writers who wrote for the ear 'could hardly have failed to put themselves in the place of the minstrel or to imagine themselves as addressing a body of listeners'. See the excellent book by Chaytor, H. J., *From Script to Print*, Cambridge, 1945.

11 The most notable exception to this generalization is the anonymous author of *Ipomedon A*, who can make something very unusual out of the tail-rhyme style: 'For were he a man of hardynes / As bounte semys and bewte es, / Be God and be my lewte, / On lyve I know non lewand nowe / That cordes so well to myn avowe / In all this world as hee' (545–50). The conciseness and wit of the first two lines are quite foreign to minstrel work.

12 On the Auchinleck MS., see Severs, J. B. (ed.), *A Manual of the Writings in Middle English*, Fascicule I, Romances, New Haven, Conn., 1967, 89. On Chaucer's knowledge of the MS., the fundamental essay is Loomis, L. H., 'Chaucer and the Auchinleck MS.: *Thopas* and *Guy of Warwick*', *Essays and Studies in Honor of Carleton Brown*, New York, 1940.

13 See Donaldson, E. T., 'Chaucer the Pilgrim' in *Speaking of Chaucer*, London, 1970; also pp. 934–7 in *Chaucer's Poetry: An Anthology for the Modern Reader*, New York, 1958.

14 Moore, A. K., '*Sir Thopas* as Criticism of Fourteenth-Century Minstrelsy' in *Journal of English and Germanic Philology*, liii (1954), 532–45. In the Prologue to *Erec et Enide*, Chrétien de Troyes expresses the feelings of a man of letters towards professional *conteurs* who 'dismember and corrupt' stories in the telling (20–2). Petrarch expresses similar feelings in *Epistolae Seniles* v. 3.

15 Mehl, D., op. cit., 256. Similarly D. S. Brewer observes that Chaucer

'bites the hand that feeds him' in *Thopas*: see p. 4 of his valuable essay 'The Relationship of Chaucer to the English and European Traditions' in Brewer, D. (ed.), *Chaucer and Chaucerians*, London, 1966. L. H. Loomis gives examples of Chaucer 'imitating himself' in Bryan, W. F., and Dempster, G. (eds.), *Sources and Analogues of Chaucer's Canterbury Tales*, Chicago, 1941, 493 note 2.

16 *Biographia Literaria*, Chapter XVIII.

17 English parallels are collected by Loomis, L. H., op. cit., 496–503; French and Spanish parallels by Chaytor, H. J., *From Script to Print*, 11. 'Listeth lordes' corresponds to the 'Oiez seigneurs' of French romances: see Gallais, P., 'Recherches sur la mentalité des romanciers français du Moyen Âge', Part I, *Cahiers de Civilisation Médiévale*, vii (1964), 479–93.

18 Crosby, R., 'Chaucer and the Custom of Oral Delivery' in *Speculum*, xiii (1938), 413–32.

19 See 'Listeth, Lordes: *Sir Thopas*, 712 and 833', *Notes and Queries*, n.s. xv (1968), 326–7.

20 Mehl, D., op. cit., 229.

21 On the 'stale adjective' *gent*, see Donaldson, E. T., 'Idiom of Popular Poetry in the *Miller's Tale*' in op. cit., 22.

22 There are four other examples of redundant 'all' in *Thopas*: 719, 773, 831 and 903 (the last being particularly awkward). Other intensive expressions are similarly repeated: 'fyn', 854, 858, 863, 881, 914; 'roial', 848, 853, 902. Chaucer uses the phrase 'goode steede' only in *Thopas*, 903. Chaucer's treatment of such expressions in *Thopas* might perhaps be compared with the 'lightly ironical' use of expressions out of older Welsh praise-poetry in the work of his contemporary, Dafydd ap Gwilym: see Bromwich, Rachel, 'Tradition and Innovation in the Poetry of Dafydd ap Gwilym' in *Transactions of the Honourable Society of Cymmrodorion* (1964), 17–19.

23 Crosby, R., op. cit., 424–5.

24 An appropriate comparison would be with *Bevis of Hampton*, 4442–4: 'Ac Beues stered him ase gode knight, / So that in a lite thrawe / Fif thosend thar was islawe'.

25 See for example Donaldson, E. T., 'The Ending of *Troilus*' in op. cit., 84–101.

26 Brewer, D. S., op. cit., 2 ff.

27 She disagrees with Lüdeke's statement 'that Chaucer's use of phrases primarily for the purpose of filling out the line is less common in his later work than in his earlier. I am prepared to show . . . that Chaucer's usage varies rather with the nature of the poem than with the period in which it comes' (art. cit., 413 note 2). Compare H. M. Smyser's study of the auxiliary *gan* used 'solely for metrical convenience' in Chaucerian narrative and not abandoned in his most mature work, though restricted there. Smyser calls this usage 'a concession – perhaps even Chaucer's greatest concession – to the popular': 'Chaucer's Use of *Gin* and *Do*' in *Speculum*, xlii (1967), 83.

28 Crosby, R., op. cit., 421.

29 'War and wys' occurs also in the *Shipman's Tale*, vii. 365. For other examples, see *O.E.D. ware* a. 5. On 'symple and coy' see Lowes, J. L., in *Anglia*, xxxiii (1910), 440–51.

30 Brewer, D. S., op. cit., 4–6.

31 Wimsatt, W. K., 'One Relation of Rhyme to Reason' in *The Verbal Icon*, Kentucky, 1954. Chaucer's rhyming techniques are documented in Masui, M., *The Structure of Chaucer's Rime Words*, Tokyo, 1964.

32 Other examples in Baum, P. F., *Chaucer's Verse*, Durham, N.C., 1961, 37. On 'rime équivoque', see Langlois, E. (ed.), *Recueil d'arts de seconde rhétorique*, Collection de documents inédits sur l'histoire de France, Paris, 1902, Index under *Equivocques*. Langlois's collection throws much light on the techniques of rhymed verse in the Ricardian period.

33 On the last, see Norton-Smith, J., 'Chaucer's Epistolary Style' in Fowler, R. (ed.), *Essays on Style and Language*, London, 1966, 157–65.

34 Brewer, D. S., op. cit., 27.

35 Lewis, C. S., *The Allegory of Love*, Oxford, 1936, 201.

36 On the Italian sources of this passage, see Bennett, J. A. W., *Chaucer's Book of Fame*, Oxford, 1968, 53–5.

37 Relevant examples, for contrast, of unhomogeneous style may be found in Lydgate's *Siege of Thebes* and in Hawes's *Pastime of Pleasure*.

38 Brenan, G., *The Literature of the Spanish People*, Cambridge, 1953, 72.

39 E. Auerbach also compares the literatures of Spain and 'another country on the fringe of Europe, namely, England' and stresses the 'popular and indigenous character of English literature in the fourteenth century', contrasting Chaucer with Boccaccio: *Literary Language and Its Public in Late Latin Antiquity and in the Middle Ages*, trans. Manheim, R., London, 1965, 324–7.

40 See Wilson, R. M., *The Lost Literature of Medieval England*, 2nd ed., London, 1970.

41 See Oakden, J. P., *Alliterative Poetry in Middle English*, ii, 'A Survey of the Traditions', Manchester, 1935.

42 The referent (beard, sea) stands to the first member of the compound (chin, whale) as the second member of the compound (garment, road) stands to an unspecified fourth term (body, horse).

43 For a different interpretation, see the note in the Tolkien–Gordon–Davis edition.

44 Examples will be found in the evidence presented by R. A. Waldron in his important essay, 'Oral-Formulaic Technique and Middle English Alliterative Poetry' in *Speculum*, xxxii (1957), 792–804.

45 Compare 417–38, where thirteen lines out of twenty-two exhibit this structure.

46 On the *Gawain* poet's use of the phrase 'see with sight', see Menner's note to l. 192 in *Purity*.

47 Borroff, *Sir Gawain and the Green Knight: A Stylistic and Metrical Study*, New Haven, Conn., 1962, 70–3. See also the chapter on style in Benson, L. D., *Art and Tradition in Sir Gawain and the Green Knight*, New Brunswick, N.J., 1965.

48 The *Gawain* poet, says Menner, 'is too good an artist to clutter his lines with formal or meaningless tags . . . The employment and the repetition of such conventional tags is so frequent in most poets of the alliterative school, that their very absence in the poems of the Gawain-group might be considered an indication of common authorship' (*Purity*, p. xvi.).

49 Borroff, op. cit., 82.

50 The statistics may be found in Kottler, B., and Markham, A. M. (eds.), *A Concordance to Five Middle English Poems*, Pittsburgh, 1966, Appendix 2, 'Head Words in Order of Frequency'. D. S. Brewer, in 'The *Gawain*-Poet; A General Appreciation of the Four Poems' in *Essays in Criticism*, xvii (1967), observes that *praise* is 'the most characteristic attitude' of the poet (138).

51 E. V. Gordon in his edition of *Pearl*, p. xxxvii.

52 See *O.E.D.* 'easy' a. and adv. 4.

53 Warton, T., *The History of English Poetry*, ii. 1.

54 *The English Works,* pp. xvi–xvii.

55 Lewis, C. S., op. cit., 201.

56 H. M. Smyser observes that Gower uses the 'popular' *gan* plus infinitive, in contrast to Chaucer, hardly at all (art. cit., 83). See also Macaulay, p. cxxvii.

57 The conversion of octosyllabic couplet into tail-rhyme may be studied by comparing *Sir Landevale* with *Sir Launfal* in the edition by Bliss, A. J., London, 1960. See Bliss's Introduction, 34–6.

58 'Enderday', used by Gower again at v.7400, is not found in Chaucer. Both Gower's uses seem to reflect the common usage of the English *chanson d'aventure*: e.g. 'Now Springs the Spray', which begins 'Als I me rode this endre dai', Brown, C. (ed.), *English Lyrics of the XIIIth Century*, Oxford, 1932, 119.

59 Macaulay, p. cxxxii. See Lewis's discussion of the revisions to iv. 1321–2, op. cit., 204.

60 Macaulay, p. clix.

61 Macaulay, p. xviii. Gower's sense of his poetic vocation is suggested by his reference to 'my muse' in viii. 3140. The only earlier English instance of this phrase is *Troilus* ii. 9.

62 On Gower at St Mary's Priory, see Fisher, J. H., op. cit., 58–61.

63 Russell, G. H., 'Some Aspects of the Process of Revision in *Piers Plowman*' in Hussey, S. S. (ed.), *Piers Plowman: Critical Approaches*, London, 1969, 38.

64 Chaucer was better placed than Langland, having at least one regular scribe working for him; but his anxieties find expression both in *Adam Scriveyn* and in *Troilus* v. 1793–6. Gower's circumstances, so unusually favourable for a vernacular writer, bear comparison with those of the 'lauriat poete' Petrarch, who usually had five or six copyists in his household, according to Wilkins, E. H., *Life of Petrarch*, Chicago, 1961, 231.

65 See Salter, E., '*Piers Plowman* and "The Simonie" ' in *Archiv*, cciii (1966–7), 241–54. 'The Simonie' is, however, very far from being a true alliterative piece. See also Hussey, S. S., 'Langland's Reading of Alliterative Poetry' in *Modern Language Review*, lx (1965), 163–70.

66 For a fuller statement of the argument which follows, see 'The Audience of *Piers Plowman*' in *Anglia*, lxxv (1957), 373–84.

67 This, the traditional account, is questioned, not very convincingly, by Blake, N. F., 'Chaucer and the Alliterative Romances' in *Chaucer Review*, iii (1969), 163–9.

68   See *Alliterative Poetry in Middle English*, ii, especially 178. J. A. W.
Bennett observes that 'the vocabulary of *Piers Plowman* is far removed from
the local and almost "precious" diction of the *Gawain* poet', 'Chaucer's Contemporary' in *Piers Plowman: Critical Approaches*, 323.

69   On 'birde', see *O.E.D.* under *burd* and *M.E.D.* under *birde* n. (1). For
examples of the coupling 'myrthe and mynstralcye', see Oakden, J. P., op cit.,
ii. 295 (N.B. *Gawain* 1952). For parallels to 'busked hem to the boure', see
M.E.D. under *busken*, 4(c).

70   Examples of 'ruddy as a rose' are collected in Whiting, B. J., *Proverbs,
Sentences, and Proverbial Phrases . . .*, Cambridge, Mass., 1968, R200. One
might compare Chaucer's equally offbeat use of 'rede as rose' in *Thopas*, vii.
726. See also G. Kane's observations on Langland's ironic use of the poetic
word *wy* 'man' in A i.61: *Piers Plowman: The A Version*, London, 1960,
434.

71   From MS. R. Compare C-text vii. 41–4. The use of a prepositional
phrase at the end of the first half-line, as in 294, is much less common in
Piers than in *Gawain* (see above, p. 26).

72   See, for example, Thrupp, S. L., *The Merchant Class of Medieval
London*, Chicago, 1948, Chapter IV, and Robertson, D. W., *Chaucer's London*,
New York, 1968, Chapter V.

73   Note, however, viii. 1158–9: 'Of gret merveile now beginne / Mai hiere
who that sitteth stille'. These words, which recall *Gawain* 1996–7, are quite
incongruous in the mouth of the confessor.

74   Owst, G. R., *Literature and Pulpit in Medieval England,* 2nd ed., Oxford,
1961, Chapter IX.

75   See Cunningham, J. V., 'The Literary Form of the Prologue to the
Canterbury Tales' in *Modern Philology*, xlix (1952), 172–81.

76   See Kane, G., *Piers Plowman: The Evidence for Authorship*, London,
1965, Chapter IV.

77   Northrop Frye, *Anatomy of Criticism*, Princeton, 1957, 40.

78   See, for example, Donaldson, E. T., 'The Ending of *Troilus*' in op. cit.

79   See Spearing, A. C., '*Patience* and the *Gawain*-Poet' in *Anglia*, lxxxiv
(1966), 305–29.

80   I am referring here to such short poems as the epistolary and moral
pieces. The case of lyrics such as 'Your yen two wol slee me sodenly' is
different.

81   In *Pearl* the employment of a complex, short-poem stanza (see Gordon,
87) in a poem of twelve hundred lines creates an 'overwrought' effect. This
is a special case.

82   R. Woolf notes in the medieval English lyric (as against the French)
'the absence of any grandeur of generalization': *The English Religious Lyric in
the Middle Ages*, Oxford, 1968, 111.

83   Arnold's discussion of Chaucer is in 'The Study of Poetry' in *Essays in
Criticism*, Second Series, 1888.

84   See Griffiths, E. T. (ed.), *Li Chantari di Lancellotto*, Oxford, 1924, 27.

85   See further the discussion of similes in Ricardian verse in Chapter IV
below, pp. 131–40.

Chapter 2

1 Woolf, R., op. cit., p. v.

2 Chaytor, H. J., *From Script to Print*, Cambridge, 1945, 85. The whole chapter, 'Prose and Translation', is of interest.

3 See the Introduction in Palermo, J. (ed.), *Roman de Cassidorus*, i, S.A.T.F., Paris, 1963. Also Stanger, M., 'Literary Patronage at the Medieval Court of Flanders' in *French Studies*, xi (1957), 214–29.

4 The early fourteenth-century minstrel Jean de Condé was among the last French poets to compose *lais* and *fabliaux* in the old manner. He also practised the new, essentially unnarrative, genres of the moral *dit* and the allegorical fantasy. See Ribard, J., *Un ménestrel du XIVe siècle: Jean de Condé*, Geneva, 1969, 11, 102, 418.

5 On Guillaume and his successors, see Wimsatt, J., *Chaucer and the French Love Poets*, Chapel Hill, N.C., 1968. Of the period between Machaut and Charles d'Orléans, D. Poirion writes: 'Nulle époque n'a peut-être été plus essentiellement, plus exclusivement lyrique', *Le poète et le prince*, Paris, 1965, 99.

6 Paris, P. (ed.), *Le Livre du Voir-Dit*, Paris, 1875. The seeds of the '*voir dit*' lie in Guillaume's part of the *Roman de la Rose*: 'Mes en ce songe onques riens n'ot / qui tretot avenu ne soit / si con li songes recensoit' (28–30).

7 The phrase 'tenres homs' occurs at l. 6940.

8 Fourrier, A. (ed.), *L'Espinette Amoureuse*, Paris, 1963, 32–3. On the relation of *Espinette* to Machaut's *Voir Dit*, see Wimsatt, J., op. cit., 127.

9 A later example of the same type is Oton de Grandson's *Livre*, ed. Piaget, A., in *Oton de Grandson, sa vie et ses poésies*, Lausanne, 1941.

10 B. J. Whiting speaks of *Méliador* as the work of an 'arch-conservative': 'Froissart as Poet' in *Mediaeval Studies*, viii (1946), 189. See also Ker, W. P., *Form and Style in Poetry*, London, 1966, 58–9.

11 See J. Wimsatt, op. cit., *passim*.

12 Fisher, J. H., op. cit., 240–2, seems to understate this influence.

13 *Voir Dit* 5256.

14 The description is by C. S. Lewis, op. cit., 235.

15 The 'Series' was so called by E. P. Hammond: see her *English Verse between Chaucer and Surrey*, Durham, N. C., 1927, 69. It may be found in Furnivall, F. J. (ed.), *Hoccleve's Works: The Minor Poems*, E.E.T.S. e.s. lxi (1892), 95–242.

16 An English account of *cantari* may be found in Griffiths, E. T. (ed.), op. cit. See also Sapegno, N., *Il trecento*, 2nd ed., Milan, 1955, 422 ff. and 619–22.

17 Branca, V., *Il cantare trecentesco e il Boccaccio del Filostrato e del Teseida*, Florence, 1936.

18 The catch-phrase occurs in *Remède de Fortune* 407, *Voir Dit,* Letters xxxv, *Espinette* 921, 3931, *Paradys d'Amours* 1604.

19 Branca, V. (ed.), *Tutte le opere di Giovanni Boccaccio*, ii, Milan, 1964, 21.

20 The highly conventional character of Boccaccio's autobiographical 'revelations' is emphasized by Branca, V., *Boccaccio medievale*, Florence, 1956, Chapter V.

21　In Prologue F to the *Legend of Good Women*, Chaucer appeals to 'Ye lovers that kan make [i.e. compose] of sentement' (69) for help in his own composition. The author of the Middle English *Partonope of Blois* says that the author of his French original 'tellyth hys tale of sentament'; and he adds: 'I understonde noghth hys entent, / Ne wolle ne besy me to lere' (ed. Bödtker, A. T., E.E.T.S. e.s. cix [1912], lines 2347–9).

22　This aspect of *Troilus* is emphasized by Lewis, C. S., 'What Chaucer Really Did to *Il Filostrato*' in *Essays and Studies*, xvii (1932), 56–75.

23　*Le Joli Buisson de Jonece*, ll. 1668–87.

24　I return to this matter in the next chapter.

25　Ed. A. Limentani in Branca, V. (ed.), *Opere*, ii. Dante's discussion of 'salus, venus et virtus' as the three most worthy subjects of poetry is in *De vulgari eloquentia*, Book ii, Chapter II. Dante says that he finds no Italian poet who has sung of war: *Arma vero nullum latium adhuc invenio poetasse.*

26　Sixth Division, *Opere*, ii, Verona, 1729, 114: 'Ma perchè fino a l'età sua [the reference is to Dante] non furono scritte in questa lingua cose d'arme, come egli dice nel suo libro de la Volgare Eloquenzia, parve a Giovanni Boccaccio trattare ancora questa parte.'

27　Ker, W. P., 'Chaucer and the Renaissance' in *Form and Style in Poetry*, London, 1966.

28　See the important article by Pratt, R. A., 'Chaucer's Use of the *Teseida*' in *PMLA*, lxii (1947), 609.

29　Dryden's handling of the *Knight's Tale* in his *Palamon and Arcite* shows that he thought his predecessor deficient in many points of epic poetry.

30　Ker, W. P., op. cit., 282.

31　See discussion in Everett, D., op. cit., 140–2.

32　*Kyng Alisaunder* is edited by G. V. Smithers, E.E.T.S. ccxxvii and ccxxxvii (1952 and 1957). It dates from the late thirteenth century. The poem exhibits, as Professor Smithers says, 'sophistication of tone and of technique', and in some ways anticipates Ricardian work; but the author is content to chronicle the whole life of Alexander.

33　The case of the fitt-divisions in *Beowulf* is controversial. See Carrigan, E., 'Structure and Thematic Development in *Beowulf*' in *Proceedings of Royal Irish Academy*, lxvi, Sect. C, No. 1 (1967).

34　This second fitt begins at ll. 833: see my '*Sir Thopas*: An Agony in Three Fits' in *R.E.S.*, n.s. xxii (1971), 54–8.

35　See discussion in Richardson, F. E. (ed.), *Sir Eglamour of Artois*, E.E.T.S. cclvi (1965), note to ll. 343–5.

36　See, for example, Hieatt, A. K., '*Sir Gawain*: Pentangle, *Luf-Lace*, Numerical Structure' in Fowler, A. (ed.), *Silent Poetry: Essays in Numerological Analysis*, London, 1970, 124–6.

37　On text-divisions in *Purity*, see Menner's edition, xliv–xlv.

38　In the alliterative *Wars of Alexander*, 'fitt' normally corresponds in the English text to 'passus' in the Latin rubrics: ll. 3203, 4018, 4714, 5626. 'Passe' occurs in the text at 2845. Compare the rubric before l. 385 in the *Sege of Melayne*: 'Prymus passus: the first ffyt', cited by Baugh, A. C., *Speculum*, xlii (1967), 25.

39　Renaissance theorists of epic in Italy disputed the relative merits of canto-division and book-division: see Hough, G., *A Preface to 'The Faerie Queene'*, London, 1962, 85–6.

40 The term 'book' used in the text at l. 1093 is not supported by any rubrics in the manuscripts, though Caxton's print has *Incipit liber secundus* etc. .

41 The story resumes in Book iii after a long Proem with the words 'Lay al this mene while Troilus' (iii. 50), where 'mene while' refers both to the time the reader has spent reading the Proem and to the time Troilus has spent in suspense waiting for Criseyde to come in. The identification of these two periods is a remarkable example of Chaucer's finesse in the handling of book-divisions.

42 Macaulay, xix.

43 Macrobius, *Commentary on the Dream of Scipio*, trans. Stahl, W. H., New York, 1952, 101 (Book i, Chapter VI). Gregory, *Morals on the Book of Job*, Oxford, 1844–50, iii. 673 (Book xxxv).

44 For general discussions, see Fowler, A. (ed.), *Silent Poetry*, London, 1970, and Excursus xv, 'Numerical Composition', in Curtius, E. R., *European Literature and the Latin Middle Ages*, London, 1953.

45 McCall, J. P., 'Five-Book Structure in Chaucer's *Troilus*' in *Modern Language Quarterly*, xxiii (1962), 297–308.

46 A. K. Hieatt in *Silent Poetry*, 122–4.

47 Hieatt, art. cit., and Kean, P. M., 'Numerical Composition in *Pearl*', *Notes and Queries*, n.s. xii (1965), 49–51.

48 See *M.E.D. above* (n adv. 1b: '(a) Higher up on the written page . . . (b) earlier in a discussion, a speech, or a story.' All the *M.E.D.* examples of transferred sense (b) are from Chaucer or Gower. Thus in *Confessio Amantis* iv. 1595 the confessor says 'as thou hast understonde above', and in the *Squire's Tale* the falcon says 'as I have seyd above' (*Canterbury Tales* v. 540).

49 Ruiz's *Libro* is translated by Kane, E. K., *The Book of Good Love*, Chapel Hill, N.C., 1968. Another example is Petrarch's *Canzoniere*, a carefully ordered selection of textually unconnected pieces.

50 For the *Traitié* rubric, see Fisher, J. H., op. cit., 83–4.

51 I refer to the G Prologue. In the F version there is no dream.

52 Deguileville's *Pèlerinage de l'Ame* is linked to his *Pèlerinage de Vie Humaine*, which it follows in many MSS., in a fashion quite like Langland's. After waking from the dream of the *Vie,* the author reflects on the perils of man's life. Thinking on these things, he suddenly falls asleep again and dreams a second dream which continues his earlier one. This is the dream of the *Ame.* See ll. 1–34 of *Pèlerinage de l'Ame*, ed. Stürzinger, J., Roxburghe Club, London, 1895. The third member of the trilogy, *Pèlerinage Jesu Christ,* is also connected to its predecessor, but more loosely.

53 On Dream ii, see 'The Action of Langland's Second Vision' in *Essays in Criticism,* xv (1965), 247–68.

54 So Gower tells the story of Alcestis as told by Zorobabel to King Darius in the confessor's story of 'King, Wine, Women and Truth' in *Confessio Amantis* vii. 1917 ff.

55 See J. Wimsatt, op. cit., 84–5, referring to M. W. Stearns, 'Chaucer Mentions a Book' in *Modern Language Notes*, lvii (1942), 28–31. In the

Pèlerinage de Vie Humaine, ll. 9–14, Deguileville says that his dream was provoked by a reading of the *Roman de la Rose*; but he gives no account of the contents of the *Roman*, and so there is no question of 'framing'.

56 L. 2525 is the last of the long lines in *Gawain*. It is followed by a final bob and wheel (five lines in all).

57 Puttenham discusses 'circular' poems under the heading 'The Roundell or Spheare' in his *Arte of English Poesie*, Book ii, Chapter XII ('Of Proportion in Figure'). The roundel 'beareth a similitude with God and eternitie'. In the *Kingis Quair*, the poet associates formal circularity with the heavenly spheres by repeating his first line, 'Heigh in the hevynnis figure circulere', at the end of the penultimate stanza (the last being a 'recommendation' of the book to Chaucer and Gower).

58 See Gordon, E. V. (ed.), *Pearl*, 89.

59 On 'repetitions' in Langland, see Salter, E., 'Medieval Poetry and the Figural View of Reality' in *Proceedings of British Academy*, liv (1968), 73–92; and on 'cycles', Burrow, J. A., 'Words, Works and Will: Theme and Structure in *Piers Plowman*' in Hussey, S. S. (ed.), *Piers Plowman: Critical Approaches*, London, 1969. Repetition is also suggested at the end of *Gawain*: 'Mony aunterez here-biforne / Haf fallen suche er this' (2527–8).

60 The poem does not stop quite here; but it is hard not to share Lewis's feeling that it should have: op. cit., 221–2.

61 An example of such a reading is Baldwin, R., *Unity of the Canterbury Tales*, Copenhagen, 1955.

62 See Coghill, Neville, *The Poet Chaucer*, 2nd ed., Oxford, 1967, 91: 'Ever since the *Book of the Duchess* Chaucer had favoured a poetry that circled back to its starting-point, one that ended in its beginnings. Now, in late life, he planned another boomerang poem, with a trajectory from London to Canterbury and back.'

63 Northrop Frye, op. cit., 163–4, discusses the significance of feasts at the end of comedies.

64 Stories of this kind do occur, notably those of Constance in the *Canterbury Tales* and *Confessio Amantis*, and Apollonius in the *Confessio Amantis*; but they are inset in works whose form is quite different.

65 *Sir Gawain*, ed. Tolkien, J. R. R., and Gordon, E. V., rev. Davis, N., note to 1008–9.

66 See the discussion in Mehl, D., op. cit., 58–68. Comparison between *Ipomedon A* and the shorter *Ipomedon B* illustrates very clearly the importance of scale in narrative.

67 See v. 267–73.

68 The average length of a story in the *Legend* is 220 lines, in the *Confessio* 150 lines.

69 Faral, E., *Les arts poétiques du XIIe et du XIIIe siècle*, Paris, 1958, Chapter II, 'De l'amplification et de l'abréviation', with references to Geoffrey of Vinsauf, John of Garland and Evrard the German. Geoffrey writes: 'vel rem brevitate notabis, / vel longo sermone trahes. Non absque labore / sunt passus utriusque viae' (*Poetria Nova* 208–10). See also Curtius, op. cit., Excursus xiii, 'Brevity as an Ideal of Style'.

70 See the decisive criticism of this interpretation in Frank, R. W., 'The

Legend of the *Legend of Good Women*' in *Chaucer Review*, 1 (1966), 110–33.
71 Griffins' eggs are in fact large – larger than eagles', according to Isidore
of Seville. I am indebted to Miss Barbara Packer for this information.
72 See Faral, E., op. cit., 75, citing Priscian, who gives as examples of
'descriptio rerum', *pedestris proelii vel navalis pugnae descriptio*.
73 Curtius, op. cit., 274.
74 See above, p. 67.
75 The whole passage is translated rather closely from the French original,
Livre de Mellibee et Prudence.
76 Lewis, C. S., op. cit., 166, expresses the opinion that 'nowhere in
Chaucer do we find what can be called a radically allegorical poem'.
77 For a fuller statement of the argument in this paragraph, see my 'The
Action of Langland's Second Vision' in *Essays in Criticism*, xv (1965),
247–68.
78 Mehl, D., op. cit., 253. See also 5, 19, 21. Robertson, *A Preface to
Chaucer*, 272–76, discusses 'exemplification' in the *Canterbury Tales*.
79 See below, p. 107.
80 On the clerical *exemplum*, see especially Welter, J-Th., *L'exemplum dans
la littérature religieuse et didactique du Moyen Age*, Paris, 1927. Also Mosher,
J. A., *The Exemplum in the Early Religious and Didactic Literature of England*,
New York, 1911.
81 See Menner's edition of *Purity*, xxxv–xxxviii.
82 Williams, D. J., 'A Literary Study of the Middle English Poems *Purity* and
Patience', unpublished B. Litt. thesis, Oxford, 1965, Chapter II.
83 Ed. cit., p. xlv. See also Williams, D. J., cited in note 82.
84 Ed. cit., p. xlvii.
85 See my *A Reading of Sir Gawain and the Green Knight*, London, 1965.
86 See Smith, B. H., *Traditional Imagery of Charity in Piers Plowman*, The
Hague, 1966, Chapter IV, 'The Good Samaritan', for discussion of this part
of the poem.
87 'Goode men' was apparently a form of address used by preachers. The
Pardoner uses it (vi. 352, 377, 904), as does the *Gawain* poet at the end of the
most didactic of his poems, *Patience* (524).
88 The God of Love also ignores 'entente'; otherwise how could he refer
to such a well-known anti-feminist as St Jerome (G 281) as an authority on the
goodness of women?
89 See Donaldson, E. T., *Chaucer's Poetry: An Anthology for the Modern
Reader*, New York, 1958, 957–8.

Chapter 3

1 Robertson, Jr., D. W., *A Preface to Chaucer*, Princeton, 1963, 223.
2 Op. cit., 284.
3 Op. cit., 285.
4 See Boccaccio's note to *Teseida* i. 5 and his allusion in iii. 18. Boccaccio's
interest in warrior-maids also appears in *De Claris Mulieribus*. See also
Petrarch, *Triumph of Fame* ii. 85 ff.

5　The reference to Judith in connection with the Man of Law's Constance (ii. 939–42) creates a slightly incongruous effect, since Constance is far from being a warlike heroine.

6　Greene, T. M., *The Descent from Heaven*, New Haven, 1963, 19.

7　E.g. Moorman, C., 'Myth and Medieval Literature: *Sir Gawain and the Green Knight*' in *Mediaeval Studies*, xviii (1956), 158–72.

8　'I cannot command the strength of Sampson nor the armed might of Hercules, but I am just as much overcome by love as they', after i. 92.

9　In his treatment of the story of Dido and Aeneas Chaucer was much influenced by Ovid's *Heroides*: see Man of Law's Introduction, ii. 53 ff.

10　Prologue, 445–9. Ed. Coldwell, D. F. C., ii, Scottish Text Society, Third Series xxv (1957).

11　Brewer, D. S., *Chaucer in His Time*, London, 1963, 165.

12　Gawain accepts the green girdle from Bertilak as a perpetual reminder of his fault: 'In syngne of my surfet I schal se hit ofte' (2433). Compare, perhaps, the poet's closing comment: 'Mony aunterez here-biforne / Haf fallen suche er this' (2527–8).

13　Spearing, A. C., '*Patience* and the *Gawain*-Poet' in *Anglia*, lxxxiv (1966), 307.

14　Op. cit., 306.

15　Spearing discusses all these cases, and especially that of Jonah, in some detail. His emphasis on comic, even farcical, qualities raises questions I shall touch on in the next section of this chapter.

16　*De Consolatione Philosophiae*, Book ii, Prosa 7, in Chaucer's version.

17　Compare *Legend* Prologue F 308 ff. with *Canterbury Tales* vii. 694 ff.

18　Spearing, A. C., op. cit., 307.

19　See Arnould, E. J., *Le Manuel des Péchés*, Paris, 1940, Chapter I.

20　See further my 'The Action of Langland's Second Vision' in *Essays in Criticism*, xv (1965), 247–68.

21　On the Sins, see Bloomfield, M. W., *The Seven Deadly Sins*, East Lansing, 1952 and Wenzel, S., *The Sin of Sloth*, Chapel Hill, N.C., 1967, the latter being especially helpful on scholastic developments. On the manuals and treatises, see for England Pantin, W. A., *The English Church in the Fourteenth Century*, Cambridge, 1955.

22　Dante derived from Peraldus his analysis of the sins in terms of misdirected love: see Wenzel, S., 'Dante's Rationale for the Seven Deadly Sins (*Purgatorio*, xvii)' in *Modern Language Review*, lx (1965), 529–33. On Mannyng, the *Manuel* and Peraldus, see Arnould, E. J., op. cit.

23　On Chaucer and Peraldus, see *Sources and Analogues of Chaucer's Canterbury Tales*, ed. Bryan and Dempster, 723 ff.

24　Payen, J.-C., *Le motif du repentir dans la littérature française médiévale*, Geneva, 1968, 455. Payen refers to Marc Bloch who, speaking of twelfth-century French romance and lyric, says: 'The whole tendency of the new literature was towards the rehabilitation of the individual; it encouraged the growth of a more introspective habit of mind, reinforcing in this direction the influence of the religious practice of auricular confession which, after having been long confined to the monastic world, became widespread among laymen during the twelfth century'. *Feudal Society* (trans. L. A. Manyon), London, 1961, 106.

25   The significance of Gawain's references to 'covetise' is a matter of dispute: see Farley Hills, D., 'Gawain's Fault in *SGGK*' in *R.E.S.*, xiv (1963), 124–31, and my own comment in *R.E.S.*, xv (1964), 56.

26   See C. S. Lewis's chapter on the *Roman* in op. cit.

27   See 'Jest and Earnest in Medieval Literature', Excursus iv in Curtius, op. cit.

28   On the Renaissance ideal, see Rose, M., *Heroic Love*, Cambridge, Mass., 1968.

29   The *Gawain* poet's humour is stressed, and perhaps exaggerated a little, in the article already referred to by A. C. Spearing.

30   Warton, T., op. cit., ii. 2.

31   Warton, T., op. cit., i. e.g. 266.

32   This interlude is printed by K. Sisam in his anthology, *Fourteenth Century Verse and Prose*, Oxford, 1921.

33   See *O.E.D. lie* vb. 13.

34   In the rather similar exchanges between Will and Imaginative in B xii, Will again uses 'perfection' as an unconvincing excuse: xii. 25.

35   See above, p. 54.

36   Neuse, R., 'The Knight: The First Mover in Chaucer's Human Comedy' in *University of Toronto Quarterly*, xxxi (1962), 299–315, sees that the tale is an 'image of different generations' and notes the parallels Saturn-Egeus, Knight-Jupiter-Theseus, Squire-Mars etc.-Arcite, etc.

37   Wise young men might even be suspected of hypocrisy (like Fielding's Blifil). Hence the medieval proverb 'Young saint, old devil'. But one pious writer calls this a 'synfull proverbe'. See Whiting S19.

38   'It would therefore be appropriate that those who are touched by hoary age should therafter cultivate chaste bodies.'

39   Here again, as in B xii. 25 and C vi. 84, the comedy concerns aspirations to 'perfection'.

40   Thus Muscatine, C., *Chaucer and the French Tradition*, Berkeley, 1957, 132–53.

41   E.g. Cunningham, J. V., 'The Literary Form of the Prologue to the *Canterbury Tales*' in *Modern Philology*, xlix (1952), 172–81.

42   The quotation is from the *Descriptive Catalogue*, issued on the occasion of the exhibition at which Blake's picture *The Canterbury Pilgrims* (in which the Host occupies a prominent place) was first shown.

43   Baum, P. F., *Chaucer: A Critical Appreciation*, Durham, N.C., 1958, 90.

44   *Convivio* IV xxvi. Dante's discussion of the Ages of Man (of which he counts four) occupies *Convivio* IV xxiii–xxviii. In *Paradiso*, Saturn's sphere is the heaven of the contemplatives.

45   See, however, Dante, *Convivio* II ix: 'That upon which the speaker doth purpose to lay chiefest stress should ever be reserved for the last; because that which is last said doth most abide in the mind of the hearer.'

46   See for example the reading in Donaldson, E. T., 'The Ending of *Troilus*' in op. cit., 84–101.

Chapter 4

1 Other examples, besides that quoted below, are i. 1087–91, ii. 764–70, 967–70, iv. 239–41. For a complete list of the seventy-four similes in *Troilus*, see Meech, S. B., *Design in Chaucer's Troilus*, Syracuse, N.Y., 1959, Chapter III, Sect. 1, note 18.

2 The simile may be compared with that in the *Man of Law's Tale*, ii. 645–50.

3 Examples are *Confessio Amantis* i. 54–7, vii. 4832–5.

4 Kaske, R. E., 'The Use of Simple Figures of Speech in *Piers Plowman*' in *Studies in Philology*, xlviii (1951), 586.

5 Another example is B xvii. 226–30.

6 See C. S. Lewis's discussion of the 'psychological simile' in Dante, 'Dante's Similes' in *Studies in Medieval and Renaissance Literature*, Cambridge, 1966, 70. There is also a 'pictorial' element in the simile in *Pearl*, since the whiteness and purity of the moon match those of the procession of virgins.

7 My evidence for calling a simile 'proverbial' in this and all following cases may be found in the valuable collection by Whiting, B. J., *Proverbs, Sentences, and Proverbial Phrases from English Writings Mainly before 1500*, Cambridge, Mass., 1968. 'Thick as snow' is no. S435.

8 Compare the account of minstrel entertainment in xiii. 230 ff. Skeat thinks that the reference is to a blind minstrel's guide-dog (note ad loc.).

9 Perhaps the nearest thing to a drastic simile in *Troilus* is iv. 520.

10 Intensive similes of this kind are common in the *House of Fame*: see also 698, 1192, 1353, 1382, 1390, 1806, 1946–7, 2130.

11 See citations in *M.E.D.* under *hound(es-fish* (b).

12 See, however, Whiting, B. J., *Chaucer's Use of Proverbs*, Cambridge, Mass., 1934, Appendix C, where a list of proverbial comparisons from *Confessio Amantis* runs to seven pages. Gower is only relatively restrained in this matter.

13 Miss Kean suggests that the *Pearl* poet's reference to gold 'sliced through' may have been suggested by Dante's simile of a newly split emerald in *Purgatorio* vii. 75: *The Pearl: An Interpretation*, London, 1967, 122.

14 *Confessio Amantis* i. 1794, 2104, ii. 847.

15 The other examples are *HF* 1605, *TC* ii. 1494, iii. 699, iv. 354, v. 1729, *LGW* F 310, *CT* i. 3472, iv. 121, 1818, v. 171.

16 See Whiting, B. J., op. cit.

Index